BUT
THAT
DIDN'T HAPPEN
TO YOU

Published by XOXOX Press
102 Gaskin Ave., Box 51
Gambier, OH 43022
xoxoxpress.com

First edition, first printing — November 2006
Printing Arts Press, Mt. Vernon, Ohio

Cover image © Ginit Marten 2006
Author photo © Anastasia Pease
Book design by Jerry Kelly

Library of Congress Cataloging-in-Publication Data

Marten, Harry.
  But that didn't happen to you : recollections and
inventions / Harry Marten. -- 1st ed.
      p. cm.
  ISBN 978-1-880977-19-4
  1. Marten, Harry. 2. Critics--United States--Biography.
I. Title.
  PN75.M28A3 2006
  809--dc22
  [B]

                              2006032089

BUT
THAT
DIDN'T HAPPEN
TO YOU

Recollections & Inventions

HARRY MARTEN

XOXOX
PRESS

For Ginit, Peter, and Tim

"What should we be without memory? We should forget our friendships, our loves, our pleasures, our work… Our existence would be reduced to the successive moments of a perpetually fading present; there would no longer be any past."

Chateaubriand
Memoires d'Outre Tombe

"Patricia embraces me on the station platform. 'The past is what you leave behind in life, Ruby,' she says with the smile of a reincarnated lama. 'Nonsense, Patricia,' I tell her as I climb on board my train. 'The past's what you take with you.'"

Kate Atkinson
Behind the Scenes at the Museum

Contents

Acknowledgments

My special thanks to Beth Ticknor, who figures in several of the stories in this book, for her support and sweet affection, and for allowing me to riffle through her memories of people, places, and events we share, however differently. And to A.M. Rosenthal, who interrupted his busy life to speak with me about a painful past that was his family history and my family mythology. Thanks to Jim McCord for a lifetime of friendship, good conversation, intellectual sympathy. For thoughtful readings and encouragement along the way, my thanks to Wayne Fields, Kit Hathaway, Mikhail Iossel, Ed Pavlić, Peter Rutkoff, April Selley, Jordan Smith, Julianna Spallholz, Ruth Stevenson and Cheryl Tucker. Thanks to Union College for a sabbatical leave that gave me time to think and write. I am grateful to Wayne Dodd, editor of *The Ohio Review*, who published a version of Chapter V, and to Guy Shahar, editor of *The Cortland Review*, who published a version of Chapter IV. Loving thanks to my father, who enjoyed telling stories, and whose voice echoes every day in my own; and my quiet mother who encouraged him, listening with tolerance and delight. Finally, thanks to my sons, Peter and Tim, for their willingness to be characters in this book, and for the pleasures of being their father; and to my wife, Ginit, for a shared lifetime of new stories, new memories.

Author's Note

About ten years ago, on a visit to my parents' California retirement home in Leisure World, my mother corrected me in the middle of a story I was telling about a broken rocking horse many, many years after the fact. "But that didn't happen to you," she said, "it happened to your cousin." I couldn't persuade her otherwise, and had to acknowledge her facts because she had been there as an adult observer while I had been a small child. Yet over a period of many decades of adult life, that memory had become one of my stories, strongly felt, implicitly believed; and it always would be mine despite the "facts." My mother, now in her nineties, has virtually lost all memories, and my storytelling truth, to the extent that it is persuasive, is what remains—for now. To some degree it can be said that all of the memories that follow "really happened," though I have sometimes changed the names, and sometimes the appearances, of the people that amble through my tales of remembering. But these memories, too, are inevitably tales of my own imagining.

I

THE HOUNDS OF MEMORY:
BY WAY OF INTRODUCTION

Lately I've been hounded by memory. I don't mean memor*ies*, so much, but the idea of the thing. That's what's yapping at my skinny heels. Oh, I have flashes alright as I slouch through my fifties, remembered moments that surface at odd times, pushed forward by a sound or image. Like the other day when I was having a second cup of coffee at Gershon's Deli after an artery clogging pastrami on rye. Sitting placidly with my friend of so many years that we don't even have to talk about our "pasts" because we've been swimming in the same warm evolutionary pond for so long, I was surprised to hear Bobby Vinton crooning on the golden oldies radio station, not wanting to say goodbye for the summer... promising all his love in a letter (sealed with a kiss). And there I was, remembering, explaining how on the weekends of a summer more than thirty years ago I'd heard that same song, hour after hour, while I was creeping in thick traffic up Central Avenue past Yonkers Raceway to the Thruway in my father's battleship gray and battleship-sized Ford Fairlane on my way upstate to date my soon-to-be wife. Or when I took my younger son out for a driving lesson at the local high school parking lot, and he asked me not to get mad if he made mistakes when he took the car out into traffic, and I abruptly found myself remembering my father's soft, urgent voice saying "watch it, watch it," as I drove perilously close to — and then up against — one of the rusting girders supporting the El subway on Jerome Avenue where I was learning to drive. At dinner, my older son who loves to mock my "noo yawk" talk says to me, smiling, singsong: "ya wanna pasdasal? Hey, tanks. Ya youzin da cah laduh?" Very funny — but half hearing him go on, I remember sitting in my childhood kitchen, looking out the window toward the brown fire escapes in the back of the house, listening to my mother telling me to "enunciate," to make sure not to let my sentences trail off and upward.

These moments aren't willed, they just bubble up. But they don't *add* up. My spots of time seem all foreground with no background, text with no context, except sharp fragments and soft feelings. Connected in bits and pieces to experiences that once seemed seamless, I find myself more and more often feeling dislocated by memory. Not long ago, my mother-in-law, having sold and closed up her apartment in Fayetteville, New York in order to live all the year round in the golden glow of Arizona's Sun City, stopped by our house with cartons of family history. Two snapshots caught me. In one, my father-in-law, dead more than ten years, looked out at the world with a young man's emphatic I-know-what-I'm-up-to gaze. Looking hard at his face on and off all evening, and many times since, I wondered who this man was whose life had crossed my own for more than twenty years before his heart literally burst. What had he been thinking when the shutter locked him in place? I hadn't known him then, of course; but looking at the bleached brown of the half-century old photo, at his fixed stare, I wished I could remember him better, could climb inside his head, could answer back for him. The other photo was much closer to home: myself on the morning of my wedding thirty-plus years ago. What surprised me as I stared into my own younger face was the realization that I probably didn't know that person looking back at me much better than I knew the person imaged as my father-in-law.

I suppose what I expected from memory was a kind of summoning of the completed past to give shape to the fluid present. Instead, the facts of the past, surfacing in pieces, seemed simply to feed the confusions of the present. But perhaps, after all, the function of memory in the present is not so much to complete or continue the past, as to invent it — putting up a fiction of "then," shaped by the needs of "now." Looking at that photo of my other self, thinking of events I simply cannot know as I knew them with my eyes and ears and tongue and feelings while they happened, circling my fragments of time and action, perhaps I am obligated not by what "was" but by what I allow to have been. Though forgetting is inevitable, perhaps the personal fictions of memory, once they are acknowledged as invention to a significant

degree, serve to gather up (re-collect) the fragments and join (re-member) them as part of a
whole body of experience.

The memories that follow, then, are not so much a
memoir as family stories assembled and recreated
from images that have failed to go away for
decades. Told and retold, they have become the
shape of the past felt in the present. Often narratives of hardship and loss, they define a confusing
human condition whose primary action is coping,
and whose primary way of coping is through determined persistence and a finely honed habit of
irony accompanied by a kind of "what can I say?"
shrug. They are about old world dislocations and
new world relocations, about finding a home and
settling a home, about growing up and growing old,
about what is taken and what is left behind. Often
focused on family tensions, they sometimes find
voice with the edgy rhythms of anger and bravado, sometime with the softer, warmer sounds of
affection, reconciliation, and healing. These are
family facts and fictions that speak of making
peace with trouble, both ordinary and extraordi-
nary, that recall identities lost and found in foreign
and familiar places, that suggest ways of finding a
path from Russia to America, from downtown to
uptown, from generation to generation.

II.

THE NEIGHBORHOOD

What Is It?

It's a flash of outfield green, seen as the El rolls by at 161st street — a window into the house that Ruth built; it's the Loews Paradise theater where starry light bulbs twinkle in an indoor sky and faux Mediterranean silhouettes are hollowed out at the edges of loge and balcony seats; it's Krums and Addie Vallins for egg creams and sundaes; it's the mirrored lobbies of the not so Grand Concourse, childhood territory of Calvin Klein and Ralph Lauren; uptown it's Alexander's; it's Woodlawn Cemetery, afterlife home of celebrities and common folk, leafy park for the living; it's the blockish glass building of the High School of Science, and the airy campuses of Fordham University, Hunter College, and NYU uptown; it's lion roars and elephant stink on Sunday afternoons at the zoo; and leafy palms in the glass and iron rain forests of the Botanical Gardens; it's tiny Poe cottage, all but lost in the concrete and brick of Kingsbridge Road; it's the handball walls and garbage-strewn sand of Orchard Beach, and the monkey bars and muddy slides of the playgrounds in Van Cortlandt Park. It smells of kosher corned beef, kielbasa, garlicky pizza, lox and bagels, boiled cabbage. It's loud with the screech of trolleys and subways, shouts from windows and the streets below — a restless place. It's the promised land of work and play for generations of new New Yorkers, upwardly mobile and spilling northeastward from Manhattan. It's the Bronx — and as all stories have a setting, this one's ours — a contrary place where community shapes identity, but where isolation grows within crowds; where insecurity energizes brag; where gossip passes as news; where a child's confusion gradually grows into knowing and memory.

Two Sewers Make the Man

One end of the block I grew up on was graced by Gold's candy store on Gun Hill Road, the other by the dog beshitten hill of 212th Street. In between, all my friends lived for the first ten years of my life. The blocks beyond were still part of the neighborhood, but they were peripheral to the cozy center of things. Kids on those other streets flowed into and out of the same crowd heading to and from P.S. 94 and 80 each day; they joined in basketball games at the Oval Playground — named for the irregular circle of its rutty cinder track — ten blocks away; occasionally they read by the same blue light in the branch library. But living in places like "The Gardens" as they did, a housing fortress with a tree or two reaching through the cement sidewalk in front, they were not quite to be trusted. They were likely to cheat at punchball, to be

Giants fans in baseball, to own their own portable radios. They were Irish Catholics with names like Brendan and Kevin, or Italian Catholics like Tony and Vinnie. They spent Sunday mornings at St. Anne's Church two blocks away. They were extrusions onto the surface of our Jewish harmonies. Of course we mocked and hated them, but more often we were together with them, feeling loyal to a place that was more important than any God could be. We lived east of Bainbridge, and together we represented our space in open territories like the Oval and the schoolyard at P.S. 80.

On most days, except in deep snow, our lives turned around the pink spaldeen ball that could be had at Gold's for a dime. We were seriously attached to these hi-bouncers that looked like skinned tennis balls but could be hit a full two sewers up the street, manhole cover to manhole cover, by power hitting stickballers like Larry Freidman; or could be bounced four fire escapes high against the building across the street by being thrown perfectly against the sharp point of the sidewalk curb; or punched the length of six parked cars by big fisted guys with Babe Ruth proportions like Richie Vacarrio. Our pockets bulged with them. We were always bouncing them as we walked, or throwing them against the sides of buildings and then chasing them up the block. When they were split by too many hits with a broom handle bat, or run over by a car that wouldn't give way to a game in progress, or accidentally rolled into a sewer and couldn't be fished out with a long wire hanger bent into a loop, or got stuck up on the fire escape of an adult with no sympathy, they had to be replaced.

Which is why Mr. Gold and his pale, pinched wife should have welcomed us as regulars when we crowded in before and after school to buy daily essentials: balls, or, occasionally, a banana yellow Duncan Yo-Yo; Topps baseball cards to trade, shoot against building walls to see who'd land closest, or flip to the ground trying to get a heads or tails match; gunpowder caps for silvery toy guns, and small missile bombs which we threw as high as we could so that they'd come down on the sidewalk with a loud pop; nickel nips — small wax bottles filled with lip staining syrup — to suck on, then chew on; black and red licorice laces which we whipped in each others' faces while we ate them; and multicolored but single flavored candy dots meant to be bitten off the rolls of paper they were stuck to. But the Golds never seemed happy to see us, as if our penny, nickel, and dime purchases were an affront to some higher merchandising scheme that they had but hadn't revealed yet. Mr. Gold was taciturn, but Mrs. Gold was viscerally and vocally unfriendly. She was sure that we would steal candy from her jumbled shelves, and of course we did. But we bought much more than we pocketed, and we were, after all, the targeted market; if we didn't buy nickel nips, who would? After school, when we weren't in much of a hurry and stood around thumbing the latest Superman or Captain Marvel comics, her weedy rasp would sound a steady sour note from behind the counter: "Hey, don't block the aisle. You think this place is a library? You gonna buy something?" Every once in a while she'd step from behind the counter to grab one of us by a shirt sleeve, and yank us toward the door, only stopping at the cash register to ring up whatever candies were in our hands.

Both Mr. and Mrs. Gold had identification numbers we could sometimes see tattooed on their wrists. We understood from our parents that the Golds were Auschwitz survivors, and we knew that we should somehow forgive them their griping unpleasantness. But what mattered was their voice in our ears, their pinch on our arms. What mattered was that they jerked us unceremoniously on our ways toward home, in no way sharing our pleasure for the products they had gathered. But home, as the saying goes, is where if you go there they have to take you in. And our parents did, along with our afternoon candy store booty — enough sugar to last through an hour or so of homework, and enough superhero images to turn a stickball game into a mythic adventure.

Where the Heart Is

I lived on the fifth floor of one of the smaller buildings on the block. Each morning I woke to the clatter of the IRT a block away on Jerome Ave., and fell asleep always to the same rhythms, staring at the slowly moving lights that slipped from the El into my window, climbing across the ceiling and down the far wall. Over and over I watched the lights, my night lights, as they carried my world away. But I have never, like the bard from Wales, awakened to find the child fled from the childless land. My Bronx will always be child-filled, though my children at six and eight years old were very ready for flight back to upstate when I took them with me one summer to tour the old neighborhood after a Yankee game. When we drove by 3544 DeKalb, my old apartment house, I could see that the main doors and windows were broken and boarded. The apparent destruction of the place, and the accompanying threat to remembered images of the place, seemed, at first, irreversible. But when we parked on Jerome Avenue under the El, and walked down from Woodlawn to Mosholu Parkway, the city came alive again. The place was as loud and busy as I remembered it, but the sweating beefy men in tank tops were talking, shouting, in a sweet Haitian lilt and a sharp staccato Spanish, mixing music and broad gesture. The Jade Garden now featured Chinese/Mex meals. Daiches Dairy was gone; the David Marcus Movie Theater was gone; the bagel bakery was gone. Only Epstein's Deli was in its old place, but the neighborhood still felt like the neighborhood, wriggling and jerking with energy. Nervous and dislocated, the boys kept a death grip on my hands; but when we were headed up Central Ave. toward the Thruway at last, they were chattering steadily about fat men and bandannaed women pushing clattery shopping carts; about the thick smell of deep frying pork; about the bright colors of store signs in languages they couldn't read; about loud trains and loud street noises. They'd felt the city, and they wouldn't forget it for years, even in the quiet of home.

Down in the Streets

Most of my childhood mornings came the same way, dark and sleep heavy. But Saturday was different, especially on hot days when street noises floated up and mixed with a radio from the living room bringing in a half hour of Buster "I live in a Shoe" Brown, and his dog, "look for him in there too" Tide, followed by a full hour of Big Jon and Sparkie, marching in to the tune of the Teddy Bear's Picnic. It was delicious there, drowsing on the edge of the woods where anything could happen, lazily coming out of a ten-hour hibernation with the jingly lines pulling you up toward consciousness: "If you go down in the woods today / You'd better not go alone. / It's lovely down in the woods today / But safer to stay at home. // For every bear that ever there was / Will gather there for certain, because, because, because / Today's the day the teddy bears have their picnic."

"You Nazi."
"You shit."

"I'll kill you."

That last part only came with warm days, but it came often enough with them to be a half-expected ritual of the day. It was the jolt that dissolved the lollipop trees and turned the teddies into grizzlies. It signaled the Saturday morning battle royal between crazy Rose and the Twitch down in the street below; and it brought us all to our windows.

Rose lived two houses up the street. That placed her at the strategic traffic center of the block, giving her a view from her third floor fire escape of all the action. The Twitch lived in a corner building across the street. His presence on the street infuriated Rose who had decided to hate the weakness of his disability, or to regard it as a deliberate mocking of her own instabilities. The Twitch, Nathan Osofsky, had a knot on the back of his head the size of a handball. He walked the block quietly, shaking violently every few steps. But he announced his coming as surely as the "I Cash Old Clothes" man who worked those streets. Nathan's signal was the clear metallic sound of a coin hitting cement every half minute. He held a half dollar in his right hand behind his back. We all thought it must have been to help his concentration. Rose saw it as an act calculated to disturb her tranquility. Every fourth step or so, when all parts of Nathan's limbs went flying convulsively, the coin was airborne. He'd stoop to claim it, settle it in his hand behind his back, and like a military man holding a riding stick behind his hip, he'd be off again.

On Saturdays the clink of money would be interrupted by the crash of milk bottles thrown as bombs from Rose's lookout. The bombs were Rose's favorite retaliation. She often used them to clear the street of stickballers and all others who threatened her sovereignty. On the block, we all walked with one eye up when Rose was in season, back from the upstate madhouse. Glass would shatter and milk explode outward before Rose's shrill voice cut the air. Sooner or later, Rose herself would descend her fire escape and take out after the offenders.

Nathan thrilled to the battle, stood his ground, traded shout for shout, accusation for accusation. And so they went at it while we all gawked:

"Hitler."
"Whore."
"Pig fucker."
"Loony bitch."

Then, serious insults.

"You Nazi. I know you. I can smell you. You stink. Your soul is stinking in your body. You garbage. You walking corpse."

"You nut hatch. Your brain is jelly-fried. They

should take you away. They should electrify your head."

"I'll get the police on you, shit head. Your clank of devil's money won't buy me."

"They're coming for you witch. They're going to tie you up, stick needles in you, shoot you up, burn you. Everybody will watch. I'll laugh on your ashes."

Eyeball to eyeball. Spit flying in great gobs. But the soft gray eyes of Marvin come between. Marvin the peacemaker. Dancing Marvin. Marvin the absent. There could be no emotional conflagration with Marvin nearby. He'd hover near a fight doing his sideways two-step, up on his toes, humming to himself, chattering aimlessly. The closeness of his persistent presence, and his complete failure to understand or respond, defused all anger. Even irrational hatreds dissolved before the truths of his indifference. Marvin's severe retardation offered perspective, a glimpse of life's real precariousness, of how impossible all strong feelings were before this vast Sahara of incomprehension. Even Rose and Nathan feel it — Rose reluctantly, but irrevocably, backing off to her fire escape fortress; Nathan shambling on down the block; the rest of us slipping back to our waking. Down in the quiet street, Marvin is left, dancing in the day.

Standing on the Corner:
Morris the Tailor, King of the Kazoo

In 1967, when I was living comfortably in California's golden glow, practicing serious work avoidance on my Ph.D. and not thinking at all about bygone days, I was stunned beyond words to discover an old neighborhood acquaintance on the Tonight Show with Johnny Carson. He was playing America the Beautiful on the Kazoo, just as I remembered him doing day after day in front of his shop on Gun Hill Road, blowing his instrument skyward, then tooting low toward the ground, like a wizened Gabriel or a sunken cheeked Dizzy, while his feet did a tiny stutter step to a rhythm that only he could hear. My wife must have thought that it had happened at last: guilt, stress, too much time spent with James Joyce and Charles Dickens, all combining to drive me round the bend as I whooped and hollered to her to come in and see THIS, Morris the Tailor, *my* Morris the Tailor, on TV all the way from the Bronx. He was, of course, the clown for Johnny, somewhere between Carnac the Magnificent and a dancing bear for audience impact. But there he was, proof positive that there's no limit to what you can accomplish in America if you're odd enough.

And Morris was odd, alright. He was no street musician, you understand, no Reverend Davis or John Lee Hooker thrashing out the blues. He was a shop keeper who'd made enough money tailoring and buying and selling stocks to send his daughter to a fancy upstate college, no mean feat in a neighborhood where 99% of the college bound kids went to City College or Hunter. His musical territory covered the small space in front of his store, stopping just short of Barney the Barber's pole next door. The Kazoo was his only instrument, and he'd hum it into high gear with patriotic songs, some Klezmer classics, and an occasional Frank Sinatra ballad. Between songs he'd talk. Mostly he talked to himself and about himself. He thought of himself as an American success story, and he was proud of it. He was a crafty guy, tickled by his sense of his own capitalist cunning. He wanted to talk stock market tips, and he didn't seem to care if he was chattering to a ten-year-old or a forty-year- old. It was a kind of cracked game of pied-piping to get your attention so he could toot his own importance and at the same time sweep the neighborhood for any possible money market advice from the business-suited men who wandered into his shop for an alteration, or passed it on their way to a haircut or the subway. Remarkably, they did stop to listen and to talk — to offer advice or hear out Morris's lamentations about his thankless child who'd moved to Riverdale and wouldn't come back to visit her dad. Perhaps they were mesmerized by the infinitely fascinating subject of the stock market, like racetrack talk or the Yankees, always worth a half hour schmooz; or maybe the peculiar melodrama of the abandoned parent, semi-crazed in solitude,

struck a chord; or maybe it was just that everyone likes a freak show.

You'd think that neighborhood kids would have
found Morris a perfect target for adolescent cruel-
ty; but in fact we were pleased to number him
among us — not exactly "one of us," like Conrad's
Lord Jim, but a figure whose genial weirdness
became for us a point of possessive pride and a
measure of the funky specialness of our piece of
the north Bronx. We all had Morris, like a secret
handshake, and there he was all those years later,
offering a bemusing late night affirmation that the
skewed rhythms of my old neighborhood had somehow become, for a bizarre moment, America's beat.

Up the Pole With Barney the Barber

Hair has always counted in my family. The story of
how Barney the Barber always asked my father —
basically bald since he was a teenager — if he'd
like a "close cut," has become a ritual, retold with
a knowing shake of the head whenever we get
together, as if to announce with resignation one
more example of the world's incomprehensible
nuttiness — to be placed alongside Eisenhower's
landslide wins, Nixon's crimes, the collapse of the
trade Unions, and the awful sure knowledge that
the more things change the more they stay the
same. Always in the background comes my mother's heartfelt reassurance that I don't have to

worry, I've got my uncle's hairline, and my uncle has hair.

Hair, thick and thin, is what brought the males of our neighborhood together for a peculiar kind of bonding experience, a sort of Jewish/Irish/Italian drum beating and sweat lodge ritual — Iron John before there was an Iron John. If women had their kitchens as a place for self-defining conversation, men had the barber shop where they'd plunk themselves and their sons down every three weeks to get cleaned up and listen to neighborhood chat.

Barney's, my father used to say, was the one place in the neighborhood where the men always got to use their heads. But making them available for tonsorial manipulation was about all they ever managed there. When you entered Barney's it seemed you left reasoned judgment behind. The shop was always tuned to the devil's radio, playing a full slate of gossip, and Barney was the DJ.

"You see that guy who just left," he'd say to the waiting unclipped peeping up over their copies of the *Mirror* or the *News*, "that poor schmuck just lost his job"; or his wife; or his son's in jail — again; or he can't stay off the sauce; or he beats the shit out of his kids; or he is "without doubt the dumbest fucker I've ever known." Barney had brass. He offered his customers melodrama to match the tabloids, and most of them lapped at it like thirsty dogs at a mud puddle, though they knew that they'd be smeared next as soon as they left the chair and headed for the door. It wasn't that they believed the stories about their neighbors' child abuse, adultery, violent discontent; it was just feel-good macho entertainment — a bar without the booze where men could be men while engaging in what might, in a different context, be an unseemly, even womanly pursuit. If the price was being on the line yourself when you weren't there to hear it, that must have seemed a small cost for the pleasures of emotional slumming in a guys' club atmosphere.

I stopped going to Barney's when my sister started dating his son. It was one thing to listen in on Barney's fictions, another to think that he might be grabbing grist for revelations about my family by pumping his kid, or by closely watching my sister when she was hanging around with him. That was ridiculous, of course. Barney's boy always appeared at our apartment door as ramrod straight and formal as a Prussian officer, his black shoes polished to a high gloss, his straightened teeth gleaming, his tie forever knotted with a tight Windsor twist. If I knew him better, or liked him better, I might have kidded him about his tightness. As it was, if I'd been paying any kind of attention I'd have at least recognized that he couldn't stand his father, with whom he probably shared nothing. We saw a lot more of him than Barney did. And besides, for Barney — and for the rest who were listening — good times in the shop depended on a heavy dose of make believe. Reality was invasive and destructive, but Barney's story-telling offered the neighborhood men an illusion of drama that was both thrilling and unthreatening. For most, an afternoon at Barney's was like an alternative family get together. Marked by familiar patterns of small triumphs and defeats, this time of shared revelations with familiar semi-strangers gave the neighborhood an oddly coherent rhythm of connection that was continually fretted, quickened, bent, by the chords and discords of the real and inviolable personal histories of family life within this small piece of the city.

I (Still) Love New York

"Don't kid yourself. *Of course* you still love New York," a friend from the Midwest says to me one day when I'm explaining how I've lost my attraction to the place, having been gone from it for nearly thirty years, almost a decade longer than I'd lived there. "Now I'm an upstater," I'd said, defining myself by the place I've been for twenty-five years. "Let's just finish the 'awr'nge' juice, and then we can take a walk through the 'forced.'" I laugh, matching my talk to the sounds of my wife, my kids, my students, who still look at me funny when I talk about an "ah-rindge," the thing that Minute Maid squeezes so well, or a "fah-rest," like the big clump of trees that borders my new house in the country.

Last summer I moved from the three story white frame city house I'd been living in for twenty-five years, a place where I couldn't help but see into one neighbor's window while I ate my morning Wheaties, and hear Dr. Dre's base-heavy hip hop drifting from the upstairs window of my other neighbor's flat while I sipped my Twinings decaffeinated English Breakfast tea. On Friday and Saturday nights I'd had no choice about listening in on the drunken lamentations and howls of rage when my redneck neighbor fought with his wife; and calling the cops to quiet the teen parties in the house across the street became a regular warm weather routine. The streets of my weary rustbelt city weren't usually loud with the noise of play or argument; and except for walking to school and back, kids didn't usually hang out on the sidewalks. Most of the action took place in the small fenced yards that were wedged behind houses, where boys played touch football, girls sunned themselves, parents cooked hot dogs, slugged down cans of Molson Golden beer, and argued about the Giants and Jets. This wasn't **the** city, but it was a city neighborhood, and it felt familiar enough to make leaving hard.

Now I'm perpetually unpacking boxes, hanging pictures, painting and scraping in a house with high cathedral ceilings, deep skylights that flood the place with sunshine, huge windows that look out on a flowing river and the rocky bluffs beyond. I'm starting to walk in the woods, and down to the river marshes, and to say things that include odd words like "my land" and "my view." I love the quiet, interrupted by squawking crows at sunset, and, down below in the water, the chug of passing boats. It is, I feel, a prerogative of growing old gracefully, and I look forward to showing it off to my sons and their families. But I find that amidst the maples and oaks, my Bronx roots reach deep; and Barney and Morris, Rose and Nathan, Mr. and Mrs. Gold, an army of friends and friendly enemies, remain — once and future neighbors, still pushing and shoving their way into my range of seeing, here in the quiet of the rural countryside. Most of all, though, I've discovered that my unpeopled landscape is ghosted by family figures, a crowd of images, voices, and memories that still say "home," no matter where I park my car.

III

THE FIGHTS

Home

"**H**oney, I'm home." Ward Cleaver has arrived; and "Father" who "Knows Best"; Desi has come home to Lucy after a long day on the conga drums; and Ozzie is back with Harriet and the boys. It's America's sitcom announcement of expected tranquility, a return to calm and normalcy after the tribulations of the world "out there." I don't remember my father announcing his presence that way when he crossed the threshold, weary after a thirteen hour work day. But I know he was glad to shut the door on hard times and aggravations. The world on the family side of the drawbridge front door, however, was sometimes no fortress of tranquility despite my mother's best efforts.

The center of the roiling was the family patriarch, my grandfather Marten, a man without a real home, both now in his isolating old age, and earlier, when he was making his determined way in a new world. His dislocations were generally self-imposed, the result of a habit of mistrust, and a sure sense that life was an unrelenting struggle that only the vigilant would survive. There was just no time for ease of affection in my grandfather's scheme of things. In place of warmth, he offered us his turbulent energy and a fighter's hardness and spirit, leaving men, women, and children scrambling to defensive battle stations during his drop-by visits which were likely to turn any sea of domestic tranquility into choppy waters.

Philip and the Fights

When I was in the fourth grade I discovered Landmark Books. Night after night, I swallowed tales of the heroes of American history: Dan'l Boone, who'd never lived in a two bedroom apartment in the Bronx, but still cried elbow room and moved on out toward Missouri; Kit Carson who circled the wagons and held off the thirst-for-blood Indians; General Custer, long blond hair whipping in the Dakota wind. Oh I was filled to the brim with it alright, and floated through days preparing to do battle with my enemies: my teacher, Mrs. Garibaldi, who proved that heads were stronger than blackboards by knocking them together; Big Julie who never missed a chance to grab the stupid peaked red wool hat with earflaps that my mother made me wear, protection against the cold but a red flag to the neighborhood bullies; Mr. Gold of Gold's candy store who disliked the kids who bought his stuff and was forever threatening to call our parents or the police. In my reading, I noticed that heroes always spent the nights before battle readying themselves, enacting rituals with a few trusty comrades to get the blood — and the blood lust — flowing. They ate big meals, drank long into the night, stared at maps of the territory, talked brave talk with friends. Impressed, I shoveled in the spaghetti, refilled my milk glass, pulled out books to confirm a military spirit with pictures of the Battle of New Orleans, Bull Run, Midway, Iwo Jima. I spent hours on the phone with my best friend Gerry, planning strategies that quickly dissolved in the face of Mrs. Garibaldi's purple-haired harangues and Big Julie's pure malevolence. As a fighter I was a nervous flop, pure and simple, Landmark Book models of American spirit and daring notwithstanding.

Maybe it was in the genes. For the most part, the men and boys of our family seem not to have been cut out in the pattern of the American warrior hero. My dad was immensely responsible; he worked two jobs, came home after 9 p.m., went off each morning at 6:30 to battle the subway rush hour, spent weekends with his son and daughter, taught them sports and to enjoy theater and music and books. He was an exceptional athlete, yet he wasn't macho, and he didn't fight. But his father, Philip, was a bit of a different story. He didn't read history; he didn't read, period. And he didn't "play" — sports, or music, or games. Matched with an ill wife and a tough job, first as a tailor, then as a Union organizer in the ILGWU, he'd had what was commonly talked about in the family as a "hard life"; and getting from day to day took all his energy. But he was a scrapper, too, and he understood the value of a good fight and of the rituals of preparation for battle.

A widower when I was old enough to know him, my grandfather rented one room of an apartment just off Kingsbridge Road about a twenty-minute ride on the IRT from our place near Woodlawn Cemetery. The old woman who had the flat took care of him in very small ways — cooked breakfast, sometimes picked up a few groceries, shared her television. But basically he was alone from Monday to Friday. He called us every other day, always brusque when I answered the phone, identifying himself and demanding my father — rarely asking after the rest of the family, never discussing or explaining himself. Except with my father, that is, and then always vigorous in his complaints, his posturing, his demands. He announced work troubles with bosses; cursed politicians; took on the mayor, the governor, President Ike — that witless wonder of Republican rectitude. His special loathing, shared by all my relatives, was for Joe McCarthy, a cross between Hitler and Mussolini on their worst days. What my angry grandfather expected from my father was not clear to me. I could hear on our side my dad making sympathetic sounds, and occasionally asking after one of my grandfather's acquaintances who'd fallen sick or was laid off or hurt. The conversations were short and tough, just like my grandfather himself. They seemed like good muscle-flexing warm ups for a weekly main event which took place every Saturday around noon when our family got together for lunch in the cramped foyer that became a dining room when my mother added extra leaves to the fold-down table in the corner. But they were just warm ups to the warm up.

Friday night was the time reserved for that true ceremony. Each and every Friday my grandfather would ring the bell at 6 p.m. sharp, announcing his coming with a loud "open up" before any of us could move. As the heavy metal front door swung inward and open, he'd brush past, leaving his hat and jacket in our hands. Living alone for more than a decade since his wife's long slow death, he seemed to have lost the art of being friendly. Maybe he'd never mastered it. Still, these visits must have mattered; he never missed one in all the years of my growing up. Settling himself in the kitchen, he waited to be waited on, accepting service as his due. He clearly enjoyed the meat and noodles set out in front of him. My mother was efficient and warm; my dad made small talk and sometimes outrageous joshing remarks, as if talking to a child. "Slow down, shorty, you'll swallow your tongue," he'd say, or "what's the matter, Pop, did you forget to eat this week?" It was the same every week, as if it had all been choreographed, rehearsed. Thinking back on it, I'd guess that the sameness mattered, the predictability seeming to announce that everything was alright for another week.

But, after all, the dinner chat was probably just a bridge to the evening's real purpose — to push back from the table and take the half dozen steps down into the living room where our old RCA was waiting with the Friday night fights. The flickering small screen featured the dance of muscled men at war: Kid Gavalan, Spider Webb, Hurricane Carter, Archie Moore, lots of guys named Sugar and Rocky. When the bell clanged to end a round, a voice hawked Gillette Blue Blades that would make us look sharp, feel sharp, be sharp, every time we shaved. Though I've forgotten a lot over the years, I've never forgotten that singsong, or the silver safety razor which screwed shut on the glinting blade with a twist of the bottom of the handle. The pitch was that Gillette wouldn't cut your face, but the order of the night was plenty of blood. It literally filled the air, droplets flying, mixed with sweat, as the rough leather gloves battered away on foreheads, cheekbones, eyes and noses. Perched on the edge of his straight-backed wooden chair, my grandfather mixed it up too, with an energy and rage that swept the room. His breath exploded with each solidly landed punch. He didn't talk through it, like my father did, or wander in and out as I did. He was steady, fixed, connected. After, the release was palpable, as he reviewed the high and low lights of the evening's card.

Philip and Ben: Blood on the Blades

The Friday night fights, a ritual flurry of surrogate battling, must have been a good tune up for my grandfather, setting a proper night-before-the-war mood of aggression and conquest for Saturday, when he would return with his own metaphoric gloves laced on for a family lunch that never failed to feature a 10-rounder with my uncle Ben, who came over from Yonkers every week with my Aunt Anne to greet my grandfather on neutral turf. Phil and Ben hated each other, and regularly said things to each other that I've never heard adults say to one another except in moments of unusual duress. My grandfather thought Ben was lazy, too lazy to husband his daughter. The family take on him also included cheap, selfish, arrogant, domineering, and domestically indifferent. On the other hand, no one had ever said in my presence that he was a wife or child abuser, an adulterer, a drinker, gambler, or even a poor provider. He simply liked to be the boss, and we already one of those — small and old and tough. Too, though family legend has it that Ben never picked up a check in his life, never drove the group when somebody else was around to use up their gas doing it, never took a family vacation, never bought my aunt or my cousins Stan and Harriet a present just for the hell of it, he liked new things and he liked to strut his stuff: his new stereo, for instance, and his huge DeSoto with its spectacular silver tail fins, simonized twice a month to a fierce reflective glow. He was proud of living out of the city in a newish co-op *near* Riverdale; and he was proud of being a shop teacher with seniority in the school system, a job he'd qualified for on the basis of work experience as a printer rather than with a college degree. He had a twitchy sarcastic humor that I liked when it wasn't centered on me or my cousins; and when I was small I enjoyed his showing off. But he was an affront to my grandfather.

In my grandfather's view, a major mistake from the days of Ben's courting my Aunt Anne was repeated endlessly on those tense Saturdays. While the Texaco Radio Opera Show filled the apartment with impassioned serenades to leading ladies — Mario to Tosca, Calaf to his Princess, Don José to Carmen — my uncle Ben's Saturday litany was "Anne, get me..." — coffee, the sugar, another cake, a napkin, the newspaper. When Ben had first visited my grandfather's home for a get-acquainted dinner, he had issued similar orders to his girl friend, and had complained vocally and steadily. But the topper, so my grandfather reminded us all many times, was the moment when Ben had refused the meal itself because there was no beer to go with it. Anne had tried to scurry downstairs to a local bar; my grandfather had forbidden it; Ben had seated himself in another room to wait. Not a promising start. Twenty years later Anne was still scurrying, Ben was still immobile, my grandfather was still seething; and we were all witnesses. My grandfather would retell this story endlessly while we ate and drank water from the tap, the punch line being a Yiddish expression that I never could quite get, but which I knew, loosely translated, meant that Ben was a selfish lazy bum then and he's a selfish lazy bum now.

My uncle's shrug was triumphantly indifferent. The hurt in my aunt's nervous chatter, the embarrassment of my mother's hurried table-clearing chores, and my father's efforts to turn the talk outward from the family navel, offered no solution and no solace. After coffee, both Ben and my grandfather seemed to take the Gillette Blue Blades out of their safety razors. There was a tsunami of name calling in English and Yiddish: *gonster macher*, *knocker*, *kvetcher*, *gonif*, lump. With accompanying dismissive hand motions and explosions of breath (feh), along with gestures of disgust — no "*rachmones*," no pity or forgiving, no forgetting — this took up an extra hour. And then calm, as if the whole thing had been an obligatory exercise in family angst — habitual, choreographed, and cathartic to boot. Both my grandfather and Ben depended on this battle royal, as if it was some sort of secular *Shabbes* ritual that both could countenance in their lack of faith in anything or anyone besides themselves.

"Religion is the world's poison," my grandfather used to say, squinting up with disgust at the synagogue near the corner of Dekalb and Gun Hill. He meant organized religion, of course. His own brand of disorganized worship at the altar of authority and control required an Uncle Ben to spar with, and a family audience for observance. Perhaps, like fight fans (or worshipers) everywhere, we, in our turn, wanted to see our gladiators punch-drunk from a pounding, though we'd never own up to taking pleasure in a family blood sport. Or maybe what we really wanted, needed, depended on, was recurrence, not completion. Ben and Philip in the verbal ring not only set the tone for Saturdays, but a rhythm for an important part of our understanding of family as a condition that's loud and fierce, conflicted, determined, undefeated and indefatigable.

IV

THE GRANDFATHER TAPES

Philip and Abe: Once Upon A Time

Twenty-seven years ago my grandfather and father sat in the living room of my father's Bronx apartment and talked together into a large gray Webcor reel-to-reel tape recorder. In order to be heard over the rumble of the Woodlawn-Jerome IRT subway and the wail of the Montefiore Hospital ambulances passing nearby, they had to speak directly into the black cone-shaped microphone. I picture my grandfather, age eighty-six and in his last year of life, concentrating all his energy and holding tight to the mike. He is talking about his life. My father prods him gently; asks questions; jokes with familiar irony. My grandfather is impatient with facts, which seem to explain nothing. But he has a firm sense of sequence and will not be rushed past essential moments. He was born — he stumbles with the first question — in 1985 — 1895 — 1885. Dates don't mean much, and names don't seem to matter, either.

"Now *where* in this wide world were you born?" my father asks.

"In Russia."

"Where in Russia, Pop?"

"In a city. A small city."

"What's the name of the city, Pop?"

"*Libashein*."

"Was that *Litvak* or *Galitzianer*?"

"*Litvak*."

The growing frustration is clear in my grandfather's voice, perhaps because he doesn't know what's expected and seems to keep getting it wrong as my father gradually pulls information out of him; or perhaps because he has his own tale to tell and names and dates are just distractions that get in the way. Perhaps, because this is his story and not history, the proper start is "Once Upon a Time." Russia is just a word to me anyway — not a mapped geography but a sound filled with vague ancestral suggestiveness. Of course I could research the matter, locate my grandfather's small city after learning how to spell it, put my pen on a map and trace back through history's boundary shifts and name changes to mark his Lithuanian location. But in the years I've had these tapes, wrapped in a clear plastic chrysalis and stored on a bookshelf among favorite stories by Dickens and Conrad, the landscape has remained as elusive and mysterious to me as Marlow's Africa. While I've always been pleased enough to say that my roots are in Russia, it seems I've never much wanted to lay them bare. What compels me are not the dirt roads and huts of the *shtetl,* or the narrow medieval streets of the cities, or even what I imagine to be the deep forests and wide fields of the countryside, but the mind and eye of the child my grandfather once was, old before his time and adrift, like no child I've ever known, in a world of work.

Once upon a time, then, there was a boy named Philip, son of an unsuccessful shoemaker (a "poor mechanic") and a sickly woman, the third of four children who survived, with two siblings dead at birth. He lived in a two room house without heat, without much light.

"Tell me, Pop," my father asks, "what kind of a home did you have? Was it an apartment? A private house?"

"Mine father," he answers, "had a house. There was no floor in the house. Just ground."

"You mean the house was built on ground, Pop?"

"I'm telling you," he says, as if talking to a child or a fool, "There *was* no floor. It was a ground. The only ground was the dirt."

"Were there any rooms in the house?" my father wants to know.

"Of course, yes. There was two big rooms. Large rooms."

All the family slept in one room; the other, which must have been a kind of outer hall, was occupied by a pig, though it was big enough for a cow, or a horse.

"So, did you have plumbing, Pop?" my father asks.

"There was no toilet," my grandfather laughs briefly, exasperated. "No water. No plumbing. There was hills. That's all."

"So you helped fertilize the grass, Pop?"

"There was pigs," he says, in an irritable voice; "pigs, they ate it up."

He says that he can't remember a time when he didn't work, but he doesn't say it that way. "What ball! I didn't know from ball," he says, when my father, teasing, asks him what he did as a child growing up in that house — did he attend school? Did he play games? Did he "play ball"? What he says, with real pride, is that at the age of seven he was a brick maker's assistant — stacking, carrying, unloading for half a day before Hebrew School. In the winter, when his father traveled for months at a time trying to scare up some business, and his mother was hospitalized for illnesses the names of which my grandfather couldn't remember, or probably never knew, he was responsible for the care of his four-year-old sister. He would come home and put a potato on the fire to feed her; he would make sure she was dressed and dry and as warm as the place would allow. Before the year was done, though, he was gone from the house himself; gone, as it turned out, for good.

"Mine father made a deal with a tailor," he says. "Thirty rubles he would pay in and I would be taught to be a tailor. But he never paid the full amount."

"Why didn't he pay, Pop? Wasn't he an honorable man?"

"Just a minute. Don't go further. I'll tell you how it was. When I went away from the house, to the tailor, I lived there. I wasn't in my home. To ten years old. I had a child to take care of. I had a cow to take care of. Every morning I had to bring the cow to some place, like a rocky field. And the cow stayed there the whole day. At night, in the dark, I used to go there and take her back. I couldn't see, and the cow was big and made very loud noises breathing. I was always afraid to do that job. Sometimes, the lady to the tailor used to give me the baby."

"You took care of a baby, Pop? Why you were just a little more than a baby yourself. What did you do?"

"I held it; I shook her," he says.

"How successful were you when you shook the baby, Pop?" my father wants to know.

"Well, I wasn't that successful. I shook her. And the baby cried. And she took her away from me."

"Ah, Pop, so it was a trick to get rid of the baby," my father says, kidding.

"Yeah, so the wife wouldn't bother me so much when I wasn't working," my grandfather says slowly, serious about the cunning victory for work-ers' rights which I'd guess he just discovered in my father's remark.

"But how many hours a day did you work there, Pop?"

"I wasn't so particular about that because I wasn't a mechanic, a real tailor," my grandfather explains. "I started in the morning and I worked until I went to sleep. Except Saturday. Then I went to synagogue; I visited my parents. At night, Saturday night, I went back to work."

"Did you have books to read?" my father asks.

"No books, no books, no books," my grandfather says. "Just the Hebrew. The Talmud. Other things. By a year and a half I was working with the tailor. They were nice people."

"Did they look after your health?"

"No, they didn't. They couldn't. I was about six months with the tailor, and then came winter. I said to him, listen, I need a coat. But he said, I need more money from your father before I can make you a coat. Mine father still owed him. Mine father was an honest person, but he didn't have the money to pay. The tailor and his wife liked me; I liked them. But they used me up. They had benefit from me. After a year and a half, when my older sister got married to a fellow from Pinsk, a blacksmith, I went to the wedding and I stayed in that city. I worked by another tailor. I was supposed to get sixty dollars a year. I made the deal myself; I was ten years old," he says with great pride.

"Was it unusual for a boy of ten to make that kind of deal?" my father asks.

"In those days, they didn't look on it like today. People worked. You started early. I was already a little mechanic, ready to live in a city. It was only ten miles from the little town where I was born, but it had everything — horses with wagons, stores, factories, a train. I felt like I was beginning my life."

Philip and the Great Bagel Strike

"It was mine first strike," he says to my father. "It was no union, just me. I wanted I should have something with mine bagel, to keep from choking. It was dry so you couldn't swallow."

He was ten years old and the issue, he says, was coffee to go with his bread at the tailor shop where he put in a fourteen hour work day. It's not that my grandfather was some poor Oliver Twist holding out his bowl for a refill of gruel. His boss was a decent enough man, my grandfather says, but a poor one too. And while you can eat and work at the same time, eating and drinking is harder to manage with clothing on your lap, and requires a stoppage. Which was unacceptable.

The way my grandfather remembers it, and he remembers it emphatically, his logic was a revelation to his much older co-workers who quickly joined him in a Bartleby-like refusal to continue. No tailor or tailor-to-be had yet choked on his bagels, of course, but they could, and that was enough to bring the shop to a halt. The details are hazy, but coffee and bagels began coming together for the tailor's three workmen and one work boy. If not precisely a triumph, it was a good start, at least, toward my grandfather's lifetime involvement with more organized workers' movements; and, in hindsight, it was a sure step toward a fated encounter with the Tiny Policeman three years later.

Philip and the Tiny Policeman

"You mean he was a short policeman?" my father asks reasonably.

"No. What short? He was a big man. But he was a Tiny Policeman. What we called him. Like a detective."

I've played the tape again and again, wondering if I heard him right. I'd never heard identity so clearly marked according to rank and character. It conjures an army of tinies: no more Assistant or Associate job titles, but tinies all: the Tiny Professor; the Tiny Superintendent; the Tiny Head of this or that.

The Tiny Policeman had come to question my truly tiny grandfather about his Socialist friends. Were his now fairly regular strikes guided by older men? Was there propaganda in his room? On the tape he searches his memory for English words that describe his bravado and his fear. This is clearly a rite of passage for him, from private to public courage, from bagels to Bolsheviks. What I hear sounds inauthentic to me, like a romance novel or a TV melodrama.

"Why did they single you out, Pop?" my father asks.

"Just a minute, just a minute. You go too far. You go too fast with this. Let me talk. One Friday, the Tiny Police came to the house to arrest me. They took me away from the house, and brought me to a police station. There was lots of detectives there. They wanted to find out who was teaching me all the things. About the strike. About the others who stopped work too. They couldn't get from me nothing. What can they get from a boy thirteen years old?"

"They yelled," he tells my father. "They waved" — he doesn't have the word for it — "a pick, a sword."

They wouldn't let him sleep. But they didn't "poke" him, or hurt him. I envision something cartoony, Tintin tied to a chair, while a villain blusters about him. My grandfather, fully caught up in his moment, rumbles on.

"They told me they'd put me in jail for years. But I didn't tell them anything, and so they let me go. When I got out, I figured it was good to get out from there. The police were on my tail ('and your tail wasn't big enough to take care of them, eh, Pop?'). I thought I should get away from Pinsk. I had a friend mine age, and we took another boat to another city, to Kiev. No Jews were allowed to be there. Any Jews coming in there, if they caught them, if it would usually take an hour to bring them home, it would now take three months, even if home was only an hour away. So, after three days, I ran from there to Katrinaslav. I came there, looked for a cheap hotel. I was at the hotel only for a night, then I looked for work, found a place. That job was worse than in Pinsk. The hours was worse than Pinsk. Everyday we used to work until two o'clock at night. It was no good. I started to strike with them, too."

"Why didn't they just get rid of you, Pop?"

"Because I was a good worker. I worked for a year and I saw it's not so good. I knew to go away to other cities. I left Katrinaslav and went to Harkov, a very Russian city. No Jews. And then, because there was no Jews, I went on to Baku."

What really happened is, of course, unrecoverable; what matters is not the event, but what my grandfather has made of it over the years, a story of shrewdness and archetypal rebelliousness, invariably honed by tellings and retellings with cronies at work, at union meetings, at senior citizen clubs, with his son and grandson. Like David Copperfield he is the hero of his own tale. And even though I'm unpersuaded as I listen, I absorb the story and the image it conjures, allowing his manipulative memory to become my own. Sometimes when I'm feeling especially hemmed in by my own caution, I haul out an image of my grandfather as a labor organizer, a fighter for worker's rights, a political child and man, even though that's not the figure I remember in my mother's kitchen, eating farmer cheese sandwiches and grousing about the toast and service.

Those were dangerous times, my grandfather says; and though he wasn't a dangerous man, he wants us to know that he danced on the edge. Before long, he says, there was a meeting in the woods with eighty-thousand people: workers mixing with police, government agents, soldiers, the curious.

"Eighty-thousand?" my father asks, "that's a very big crowd, Pop."

Especially for the woods, I'm thinking. Where did they put the trees? My grandfather offers no particular details. Listening to him, I can't conjure up the sights, sounds, or smells of the place. But while he talks, my Movietone imagination flashes images in black and white, somewhere between Keystone Cops and Battleship Potemkin. I see my grandfather scurrying back in the night through the narrow streets of Baku to burn his library of socialist literature, pamphlet by pamphlet, book by book, in the small stove of the apartment he shares with other garment workers. He knows the police will be rounding up troublemakers, and he doesn't want to be swept away. He is now fifteen-and-a-half, has met and courted the woman he wants to marry — the grandmother I never saw and whose name I don't even know now; and in order to protect himself and their relationship he will take to the road, doing piece work as he travels. He has recently passed a state test to prove his tailoring skill, and because the government needs work done on clothing to outfit its army and civil service corps, he has been given "papers" and will be allowed to move through many towns that are normally shut to Jews. What my grandfather hasn't reckoned with, though, is military conscription into the Czar's army where Jews have, for generations, provided cannon fodder in European wars.

Philip and the Train to America

My grandfather never liked his older brother. In all the years of my growing up, he never once uttered his brother's first name. When he was mentioned at all, it was always with immense disgust as "that *gozlin*, that swindler," and sometimes when especially dismissive, "that *paskudnyak*." There were many bones of contention, the largest being the brother's siphoning off of my grandfather's share of a business partnership so that he could keep a fancy lady on the side — lying all the while to his wife, claiming that my grandfather had failed to pay the cash into the business that he had promised. It wasn't ordinary sibling rivalry, then, but low-level deceit that separated the two. But it wasn't until my grandfather reached back into memory while he talked with my father into the tape recorder, that I understood just how far back the brotherly resentment ran, preceding financial dirty dealing, preceding even his brother's arrival in America, a trip that my grandfather had sponsored and paid for.

As my semi-socialist grandfather tells it, it wasn't political pressure that drove him from his not very nurturing homeland, but the common pressure of family dynamics. On the road, but not on the run, after the scare which followed his political activity on behalf of workers' rights, my grandfather was pushed out of Russia by his father's preference for his older son. Privileged by his seniority, this brother was understood to be the "scholar" of the family. He spent his days studying the Talmud, gathering more sophistry than wisdom, my grandfather implies. Learning to split the finest hairs while my grandfather was learning to pull the coarsest threads, he learned, too, the fine art of self protection. And so it was that my grandfather found himself put forward as the older son, his brother the younger, when the Czar's army reached into the family for a draftee. This meant, of course, leaving Russia completely; and while my grandfather isn't clear on the details, what he remembers is that he was helped across a border into Germany, traveling then "by cattle boat" to London, "by train" to Canada, and by boat again to New York. My father, who has been needling the facts out of my grandfather for hours, lets this pass. He simply listens, as my grandfather elaborates on the joy he felt in dancing and whooping in front of the border guards from the apparent safety of his first new freedom in Germany; as he describes the immensity of the darkness and the intensity of the cold of London which he hated; as he boasts of being the only one who wasn't sick in the hold of the boat which carried him from somewhere to somewhere else, he can't remember exactly; and as he explains his relief and readiness as he stepped down from what he remembers as a train, in Canada, where he recovered for a few days before continuing on to New York City, the place he wouldn't leave for more than a few days at a time for the next sixty years.

Greener, Come Here

"Hey greener," he says to my grandfather, "come here." I see a "Spy vs. Spy" scene from an old *Mad Magazine*: a whisper from the shadows drawing my grandfather in as he steps out onto the streets of New York for the first time. But it's more like a street vendor hawking the bargain of a lifetime, a first brush with capitalism in the green and golden land of the free: "Psst, hey, have *I* got a deal for you." He offers to carry luggage and navigate the 3rd Avenue El and crowded streets. But what he's really marketing is a sense of order to replace confusion, calm for fear. For four dollars each, he says, he'll take my grandfather and three other green shoots just off the boat, all presumed fresh and tender with inexperience, to their *landsmen* where they'll spend their first nights before looking for more permanent rooms and a job. Though tired and anxious, my grandfather is proud of his savvy; and, as he explains to my father, he was not about to pay the going rate for help which he felt should be a kind of good neighbor courtesy to newcomers. Chuckling, still delighted with his triumph over all enemies, he explains how he chopped the price to seventy-five cents, accepting, finally, the plaintive logic of the would-be porter who wondered how could it not be worth so little to find your way into the darks and deeps of the city, to be taken "home" without even having to carry your own old country baggage. Echoes of the bagel strike ring in every word.

"I went with three boys I knew from Harkov and Baku," he says. "In Canada, in the middle of the night, some Jews took us in. They gave us eat and enjoyed us. They sent telegrams. Like a reception committee. It was a nice place, and they treated us very nice. I had one suitcase; everything I owned. Some society, I think they were. Toward evening, they brought us to a ship to go to the United States. It took maybe a day. Every place we used to come, people used to come and take us. In New York, too, but they was crooks. They took us from the boat to a little office and they asked for the money to take us to a place to stay. We started to walk with them, and I said to the boys why do we have to carry the valises? Let them carry it. We put the valises down on the corner and we didn't move. They came down in price to two dollars. The boys agreed and went with them. One person stayed with me. I didn't want to give him the money, but when I said I'll pay seventy-five cents and no more, he held out his hands and smiled and said OK."

My grandfather is preening in the memory of his triumphal moment, but city boys will be city boys, and my grandfather's guide had surely been up this road before. Walking him to the El train, up the long staircase to the platform, he told him to get off in two stops and vanished. Spilled out into the city at Elder Street, my grandfather — unable to talk with anyone in America's language, hauling his own valises now, wearing a cap like a policeman's and a red shirt that announced his politics — held his cousin's address out to passers by like a lost child. All pretense of bravado collapsing before that memory of helpless dependency, my grandfather softly tells us that all he could do as he tried to find his way was walk "like in an ocean," swept by deep waters. Washed ashore at last, my grandfather came to rest in the walkup near Essex Street where his cousin slept. When he tells it, the arrival sounds like a ritualistic welcome for a hero, complete with an initial greeting by a gathering of women, a cleansing bath where, as he says, he could "wash around himself," and a banquet of Challa, a soup thick with schmaltz, and boiled chicken. But beneath the tale I can hear grating tones of frustration and not-so-splendid isolation.

By the end of the next day, like an American hero, my grandfather had moved on — found his own place to live, the windowless living room of a two room rental which he shared with another new "boy." With a sink in the hall and a toilet somewhere "downstairs" in the yard, it serves now simply as a kind of launching pad for stories of rocketing success. What my grandfather offers to cover his first year in America is mostly a litany of new jobs, pay raises, roomier apartments, small acts of defiance. It's Vanderbilt on a pygmy scale, and the stuff of Americana bootstrapping stories from Alger to Dimaggio. The man my grandfather must have been becoming is lost in it, though, usurped by the image he wants to project to his son and grandson half a century later, and by statistics of success: from three dollars a week to forty-eight dollars a week in barely a blink; from button holes to "the whole coat complete"; from the frigid toilet seat to the ah! of indoor plumbing, hot and cold; from the stink of Delancey Street to St. Paul's Place in the countrified Bronx, where there were still farm fields, and where a mounted policeman was only seen once a week; from humiliation to achievement.

And the Leaves That Are Green Turn To Gold

When my parents visited from California where they deeply enjoy their retirement near Laguna's beaches, I found myself complaining about my grandfather's unwillingness or inability to discuss his family life in America. The closer his taped conversations got to the present the less he offered. Perhaps he thought that my father knew all about this part of his life anyway. Or perhaps it was too personal, or too painful. Or perhaps it simply wasn't essential to his sense of himself in these years.

My grandmother is mentioned, but only as a shadowy figure here, sent for from Russia, married within a year, suddenly but steadily ill for many more than ten years, then dead at fifty-three from a heart weakened by early childhood illness. My grandfather concentrates on their earliest years together in this country, when he believed he still had some control over their destiny.

"I had a lot of greeners to take care of," he says. "First my girl's brother. Then my girl. He ran away in 1904 to get away from the war of Russia with Japan. My sister's husband also ran away from the war. The Jews who could, ran away. They came to me. When she came here, I didn't want to get married right away, so I told her to say I'm her cousin. When she came to Ellis, I was late to meet her, and I didn't see her. She had to stay overnight. But I went the next day, and they wouldn't let her go with me, only a cousin. I had forgotten that her brother was here. So I said that he should go down there, and we took her to a friend of mine, got her a shower in a public bathhouse, took her out for shopping to get things. I took her to my cousin in Delancey Street and bought her skirts, dresses, coats. I spent some money on her."

"Just out of curiosity, Pop," my father interrupts, "how often did people go for these baths? Every day? Once a week? Twice a month?"

"Huh," he says, "not everybody went at the same time. Some could go every two weeks, some could go every month. If you wanted to take a bath you could go there."

Then he's back on track. "So I ordered some clothes for her, shoes, other things. She rested a few weeks and began to look for work. She was a dressmaker. It was a very bad time for work. It was 1905, and she couldn't find anything for one year. After three months I got her out of the place where she was, and brought her to the same apartment where I was; the same apartment but a different room. Also there was a father and a mother and two daughters there. All the greeners who came from Europe and didn't have any money to get a place, lived in rooms in other peoples' apartments. The poor people all lived like that. We'd come together for supper. But mommy wasn't doing anything. She used to go around with some of her friends from Baku, all day around the 7th Street Park. She didn't eat all day, just a glass of milk. I used to fight around with her, why she didn't eat. We were there together a year, and I made up my mind to get married. What sense did it make that she should suffer like that? So just when I made my plan to get married, then she found a job. She worked a week and made ten dollars. I said, that's enough, we're going to get married. I had saved a couple of hundred dollars. I took three rooms in Cherry Street. We got married in the same rooms."

"Did you get wedding presents?" my father asks.

"No presents. No gifts. What gifts? And then we started married life. Three rooms on the fifth floor. The toilet was in the hall."

"Did you have hot and cold running water, Pop?" my father wants to know.

"No water. Nothing."

"No water at all, Pop, or just cold water?"

"Water. Yes, water. Cold water. No hot water."

"I fixed up the house," my grandfather continues with some pride in his resourcefulness, "but I couldn't afford a stove. I didn't have enough money for it, and I didn't want to take by peddlers. I didn't want to spend money that wasn't mine. Everything I want to buy was the cheapest kind, but not by peddlers. I want it to be my money. Three months it took me to save money to buy up the stove. It was winter, but in three months it became a light house, a warm house. She didn't know how to cook; she didn't know nothing. But she learned."

His voice getting quiet, my grandfather explains that by the time they got to the woodsy Bronx — with upward steps along the way at Monroe Street, 121st Street between Second and Third Avenues, and 120th Street in a garage across from a stable — my grandmother was starting to get sick. "And I start to get the business with doctors," he says.

A few poignant sentences suggest hurt and helplessness: "Mommy was sick all the time. Maybe if they took the tonsils out when she was a child, maybe it wouldn't come to that. Maybe she would still be alive until today. All I could do was put hot bags on the heart. And that was the whole business." My grandfather does not elaborate. He names the places where my father, my aunt Anne, and my uncle Carl were born in the Bronx, but provides no glimpse into his relationship with any of them. He talks only in the broadest terms of decades of work and then of retirement years spent sitting with members of the Kingsbridge Road Senior Citizens' Club, or watching trials in the Bronx County Courthouse where judges, lawyers, and clients all struck him as shysters. I want to know what my grandfather was feeling during the years he was defining himself by his climb to financial security. My mother says, "but that *was* his life, all of it."

Not long after my grandfather died, my father gave me a magnificent gold Waltham pocket watch that he said had been the first thing of real value my grandfather had bought for himself in America. It runs five minutes fast a day; the long minute hand, tapering to a kind of ornate arrowhead, frequently catches on the small second hand that turns round inside its own small circle.

V

GRANDMOTHER LOVE

And the Women?

"**W**hat about the women?" my wife asks, when I talk with her about my dip into this stew of storytelling and memory-making. "It all sounds pretty patriarchal to me. Where are the grandmas, the moms?" She's right, of course. But in my family I've always found the men more visible, more obvious. As if assuming a right of birth, they have been the spinners of words, the arguers, self-proclaimed solvers of personal and public crises, shapers of lore and legend. In the weekly get-togethers for meals or celebrations, the women have always seemed singularly silent, at least in the presence of men. It's not that they've been shy or deferential, I think, just not especially interested in talk, and so not as immediately available to the tall tales of my memory.

When my mother heard that I was projecting some sort of writing on family memory and tale-telling, for instance, her first and final response was "thanks, but no thanks." She'd provide coffee, fruit, and cakes, but leave the chat to the men. Still, while she dodged questions about her life, proclaiming that "there's just nothing to tell," she was willing to be a sounding board for my own recollections of my biological mother's mother, and to clarify moments of my step-grandparents' lives. For if the family matriarchs as I knew them weren't storytellers themselves, they were surely authentic stories in their own rights.

In the Soup Kitchen

My grandmother was the least happy person I have ever known. Living just across the street and up the block, near the corner of Jerome Avenue and Gun Hill Road in the Bronx, she hardly ever visited our apartment after my mother died. But she was a looming presence, declaring her moods and needs regularly with insistent phone calls that sent my stepmother scurrying into the neighborhood to pick up groceries and set up services with dry cleaners, hardware store owners, handymen, who had all too often been verbally abused and offended by my grandmother. There seemed to be no pleasures in old age, and my grandmother's fretful unease was daily visited on the rest of the family.

I moved through the battle zones as willfully oblivious to the mine fields, skirmishes, and truces as I could be. I loved my grandmother because she was my grandmother, but I took little interest in her life. Still, family obligation is family obligation, and each Sunday morning for years my sister and I would be sent across the street by my parents to visit with this solitary woman who had outlived her husband and many of her daughters, and who would feed us and lament steadily for her lost family, complaining all the while about the hardness of those who remained.

My grandmother lived in the largest, oldest building on the block. With two six-story sections facing a central courtyard, it was probably once the queen of the neighborhood's apartment houses. But it was a dirty hulk by the time my grandmother came to be living there, its white and brown bricks blackened by decades of city grit. The lobby, which could only be entered by buzzing the apartment you wanted, had broken red-tiled floors, a wall-sized mirror framed with strategically placed metallic light fixtures, and a stink of grease from cooking that hung in the air perpetually. The elevator was a child's delight, with great round buttons and a brass accordion sliding door that had to be slammed shut before the thing would budge. But the hallways were dark and airless, the floors covered by dusty carpeting, and the numbers on the heavy steel apartment doors indecipherable with age and shadow. My sister and I well knew how many doors down from the elevator to go, and knew my grandmother would be expecting us.

Coming in just after breakfast, we'd stay through lunch which was always the same: *lokshen* soup — boiled chicken with skin and meat, and a few bones, floating up to the top along with the thick broad noodles that were the best part. Most, but not all, of the fat was skimmed to be placed in a large glass jar which every few weeks was sent home with us, hot with the latest addition, to be thrown out by my mother, or to be pulled out when my father's father demanded *shmaltz* for his bread during his Saturday morning visits. Compelled by the steady refrain of "*ess meineh kinder*," my sister and I would pick out what best bits we could, listening to the rumble of my grandmother's Yiddish upbraidings and regrets, mingling with unflappable outpourings of her real love for us gathered in urgings for us to take in more and more of the thick nourishment.

Having lived in Canada and New York for more than four decades by the time I knew her, my grandmother steadfastly refused to speak English which she seemed to understand perfectly well and which she could slip into and out of when she chose. As a result, she seemed impenetrably mysterious to me, half understood at best; and in her shadowiness she took on almost mythological complexity as I grew older. The broad outlines of family history have always been clear and recoverable, but the nature of my grandmother's personality within that history — her motives and needs — remains hidden from me by words which I'm not sure even today I understood when I listened week after week.

I never knew much Yiddish. But I *feel* that I knew what my grandmother was saying to me Sunday after Sunday, her meaning caught in her cadences and inflections if no way else, though there was rarely a chance to ask questions and have her answer back. Both protected and defeated by her linguistic withdrawal, my grandmother took charge of her environment, shutting herself into a space she might control in a world that must often have seemed hostile, and in the process shutting herself out from full family sympathy here in her new world.

Listening to the rise and fall of my grandmother's voice, and watching her expressive sorrowful face, I knew when she was angry and when she was resigned; I knew when to commiserate with her, clucking and tsking, but quietly so that it could be taken as throat clearing if I turned up wrong with my reading of the perplexing monologue. When she laughed I smiled back; when she grimaced or frowned I made sympathetic sounds. I caught names of people I knew — uncles, aunts, cousins, parents, and I put them together with her tonal and visually expressive moods. I recognized when she was in full stride and when she'd reached a pause. And I knew when she was turning her discontent in my direction, or my sister's, as if we had been her last resort in the family court and we'd let her down with our incomprehension or indifference. While the soup congealed, my sister and I listened hard, straining to keep focused on the foreign sounds and to make some precise sense of them. And when the lunch hours had rolled by once more, I left feeling that I'd understood my grandmother. But if my father had asked me exactly what she'd spoken about, I don't know that I'd have been able to tell him.

Like a Rag

"Harry, Harry," my grandmother would say as she dished the soup, invoking my long dead grandfather but momentarily confusing me with my own name, "if you could see how they treat me. Like a *shmatte*." I suppose she meant my aunts, my parents, my sister and me, neighbors, old friends in the park, the man who ran Daiches Dairy on Jerome Avenue, the vegetable grocer on Gun Hill, any and all who, crossing her path, seemed to her to be using her like a rag to wipe their shoes with. In the loneliness that was both willed and came willy nilly, she didn't distinguish between the indifferent masses and the few who paused to hear her out, to visit, to help.

I don't know if my grandfather would have been a good listener. My grandmother sometimes seemed angry with him for having died suddenly. I don't remember having seen any photograph of him, or having any family member talk of him with any sense of his presence. Knowing nothing, I took the fact that he once was a fur trapper in Sault Ste. Marie as my own link with some sort of frontiersman inheritance, while ignoring the ordinary proportions of his death after a fall from a scaffold while he was working as a house painter in Brook-

lyn — the only other fact I knew about him. I had
no idea where Sault Ste. Marie was, or what it was,
but the sound of the place conjured wild Sioux war-
riors; and my grandfather's occupation put him —
and me — closer to my TV heroes, Davy Crockett
and Dan'l Boone, than I had any right to hope for.
My grandmother, though, didn't seem to figure
much in my version of my grandfather's bold psy-
che. Left to cope, she hadn't coped well with the
loss of an authentic house painter, while the early
death of my fur-trapping frontiersman only fed for
me the image and the myth. Her anger and pain
simply washed over my fantasizing imagination.
Centered on myself and my images of myself, I was
unempathetic, confirming how very alone she must
have felt.

Night Lights

But it wasn't just that the reality of my grandmother's life failed to fit the unreality of my
childish imaginings. What little I could grasp of
her unhappiness was confusing and frightening.
"Pray," she'd say to me and my sister, "pray that
you won't ever have to endure all you can learn
to bear." The not-so-subtle implication, of course,
was that she *did* endure it all, which was a heavy
bit of baggage for a nine-year-old and a twelve-
year-old whose burdens rarely extended beyond
the slow movement of time on these Sunday
mornings. But after lunch one day, beside herself

with grievance and fear, she showed us a light into her darkness.

The living room windows in my grandmother's flat looked out on the upper part of DeKalb Avenue. The synagogue was in full view across the street, and you could see action out toward busy Gun Hill Road if you leaned out a bit to the right — cars in a steady flow, shoppers headed toward Jerome Avenue, pulling compact wire-cage shopping carts with small red wheels, girls hopping through a pattern of boxes chalked on the sidewalk, stooping to pick up keys or jacks as they went, and my friends playing car-dodge touch football and stickball. It was all noise and city pageant and my grandmother loved it. But from her bedroom window there was nothing to see, and no street-noise drifting up to break the silences of her solitude. The heavy double hung window faced a narrow inner courtyard, and looking down into the thin rectangular space was like seeing through the wrong end of a pair of binoculars. The space between the brick walls wasn't big enough for anybody to sit and talk in comfortably, or play in, or even walk through. Occasionally a bag of trash would land at the bottom of the shaft, which made it seem like an incinerator. But for the most part, you just didn't look out in that direction because there was nothing to be gained by it.

That's why my grandmother's outburst was so surprising and disconcerting when one Sunday afternoon before we were on our way she took me and my sister to that window and asked us to look out and tell her if we could see the Nazis. They were shining lights in her windows every night she said, keeping her awake; and though she couldn't see them, she was sure they were following her out of the building when she went shopping. Just after she fell asleep they'd begin with the lights, she said, that would push through the curtains and shake her awake. She was too frightened to look out, though she'd get out of bed and stand behind the curtains and yell out to them to leave her alone. They'd keep the lights on for hours. Every night. She didn't know why they hated her so much except that they hated all Jews; her friends weren't being hunted like she was.

When we looked out, all there was to see were the windows of other apartments which, like my grandmother's, faced onto the inner court. Their lights turned on at evening must have been the sinister enemy spot light. When my sister and I tried to explain what seemed obvious to us both, my grandmother said she would not be fooled, and was not to be consoled. Giving us a resigned hug at the door, she told us we would understand some day. "Everything ends with weeping," she said – "*altsding lozt ois mit a gevain*" — giving us a soft push toward the elevator, which we were glad to step into and ride down to the welcoming street below.

Relieved to be back home, we told our father about the morning and called our friends to play. What he did or didn't do, we never asked. Old age and loneliness sometimes change you, he said to us, but we couldn't even begin to comprehend the idea of age. In long hindsight, I assume he talked with my aunts and uncle, and with my grandmother. Perhaps he talked with her about frightening the kids, about neighbors, about the "real" world. But I doubt that; it would have been out of character for him to lose patience or respond without deep sympathy. Perhaps he and my aunts bought darker curtains. Perhaps he scoured the area for Nazis, and offered protection. Perhaps, after all, he simply went over to her apartment and offered what was most needed, comfort and attention. We didn't go back for a few Sundays, but when we did, all was back to normal: soup was soup, complaints were lively, and my grandmother's food driven love for her "*shayner maideleh*," her beautiful little girl, and her redheaded "*boychik*," cast a stronger light into the dark than any night lights from a courtyard window.

A Thing of Beauty

My grandmother loved beauty — full-blossoming, extravagantly costumed, glittering beauty. Her apartment was painted a standard fifties drab beige, and her slipcovered sofa was an overstuffed pale brown floral thing; her kitchen table was white speckled Formica and her kitchen chairs were neo-Bauhaus modern with off-white plastic seat covers and tubular metal frames. But the massive mahogany brown RCA floor model TV, a gift from her children, was tuned steadily and exultantly each night to a variety of Variety Hours. She took an immense, almost personal, pride and pleasure in the dancers who high kicked their way across Ed Sullivan's Sunday night stage. She oohed and aahed and clucked over the sequined grace and strength of the circus acrobats who formed mighty human pyramids with a small blond at the top, or tumbled through the air into one another's arms, swinging high above the gasping audience. The singing barber, Perry Como, dropped in weekly to fill the quiet with croonings about romantic places and stars-in-your-eyes emotions. My grandmother appreciated the hummable melodies and the soft imaginings of places far from the many hard landscapes and mindscapes she had passed through on her way, finally, to her two and a half rooms in the Bronx.

Piano accordions were popular in our neighborhood; every family had at least one child squeezing through "How Much is That Doggie in the Window." But Lawrence Welk's TV Band, which drifted into the neighborhood once a week, had the biggest Hohners and fastest fingers around. My grandmother would tap along to the Swedish Polkas and bask in the soft mists of "Autumn Leaves." Her greatest delight, though, was reserved for Liberace. She absolutely loved Liberace's glittering gold suits and the cande-labras flaming near his piano. He was gorgeous; the light bouncing off the pure white wall of his smile could blind you, and a half an hour in his radiance went a long way toward carrying my grandmother out of her dark corridors of memory and confusion.

But beauty couldn't always tame the beast that shook my grandmother's mood. Sometimes that Keatsian "joy for ever" was bitten off in a moment, hardly a satisfying mouthful; or it was snarled off impatiently, as if its very existence in so much misery was an affront. Sometimes my grandmoth-er, as if in disgust and self-punishment, would watch her show of shows with the sound shut off, or sit staring at a darkened screen with only the voices and music reaching her. Or she'd simply refuse to flick on the magic box at all.

There was no reasoning with my grandmother's moods, and no fooling with them, either. One Moth-er's Day, my mother decided to buck the trend of providing an unimaginative gift. She'd found at Lord and Taylor's a magnificent set of beautifully decorated playing cards. There was a Bonnard-like beauty to it, a garden picnic scene vibrating with deep sky blues and electric yellows, softened by washes of moss green and pink pastels. The idea, of course, was just to have the cards around, to soak up their prettiness or put them away as the spirit moved you. My grandmother's response was visceral, immediate, and nasty. No thank you. Take them back, or throw them away, she didn't care which. What did my mother think, that she was a cardsharp? A gambler? Her daughter, the real mother of her grandchildren, would never have treated her this way. She made a ruckus, a stagy affair that probably had some kernel of real hurt in it — in the reminder that her daughter was dead and had been replaced; but it was mostly just for display and my mother knew it. She had taken a gamble herself and lost, and she wouldn't sit down to play at cards again anytime soon. Next time it would be dish towels or Mums. Liberace's reign of loveliness would have no more rivals for my grandmother's attention, and beauty would continue to dance into the Bronx drab of her apartment only as *she* willed it, in half hour bursts from NBC or CBS.

She Only Cried Into Her Pillow

"But who *was* she?" I ask my sister one evening on the phone, as if we've ferreted out all the obvious commonplaces of identity and she still eludes us, this matriarchal mystery woman. In fact, we've hardly made a start — a semi-willful avoidance on my part. We've been talking about Mrs. R., as my grandmother has come to be known by us with some amusement and some discomfort. Wanting to keep her at an emotionally safe distance, we refuse to allow her a personalizing name. Our conversation about this stolid and stubborn long-lived presence in our lives is something we've managed only two or three times in thirty years. And I find that even as I push my sister toward the subject of family memory which has been on my mind for months, I'm still trying to avoid specific images of the unhappy old woman who once greeted me at her door with the melancholy declaration, "I only cry into my pillow." Predictably, I had backed away from the waves of misery that roiled around her during my growing-up years; and predictably I felt guilty about that as I grew into my own family responsibilities. I want to understand her now that I have distance, but I don't want to wrestle with my refusals to know her when I had the chance.

My sister and I agree that Mrs. R's defining characteristic for us was her affectionate morbidity, a loving but self-centering gloominess that refused all solace. But, we agree across the phone lines, there must have been some who "knew her when," who remember a sunny side, before the relentless unhappiness wrecked her spirit and good will. What I want to find is the grandmother I never had, never knew, not the one I can only look at out of the corner of my peripheral vision.

It occurs to me that it's time to call my uncle, who might be able to offer a different view of Mrs. R. An immensely tough and successful journalist with a strong sentimental streak, he has always seemed glad to reconfirm our connections. When I tell him what kind of talk I'm after, he invites me down to the city for a lunch and a rummage through our collective memories.

An Adventurer

When I arrive at my uncle's apartment, I notice photographs on bookshelves, tables, walls, everywhere. The faces are familiar to me from TV, newspapers, and book jackets — stars of all kinds who inhabit my uncle's life intimately. But the pictures that most intrigue me are the old brown ones I noticed immediately — of my grandmother, the man I take to be my grandfather, the klatch of small and squirmy children that are draped on laps and over chairs and each other. One photo in particular stops me. In it, a small man in a dark suit and a squat bulky woman in a shapeless plain dress with a rounded white collar look straight into the camera, while on either side of them and at their feet a handful of bored girls look away. In the corner, a five-year-old seems to be pulling angrily at a stocking which has slipped down. I'm struck by the magisterial formality and serenity of the parental pose, the straight ahead stare that unequivocally says "I am."

I expect my uncle to offer wistful impressions of his mother as a grand figure who held the family together, a nurturing conscience keeper, source of unequivocal self-sacrificing love, who suffered through her children's and husband's moods. I suppose this is the picture I've come for. Instead, standing in front of that family photo of nearly a century ago, he begins:

"Harry had style. Sarah didn't have any at all."

Surprised, I'm about to make some odd apology on her behalf, forgiving her shapeless bulk and drab gown in light of how hard it must have been to have "style" while looking after five daughters in an absolutely unforgiving frozen foreign place like Canada — when my uncle continues: "But she was an adventurer — Harry's pirate queen."

"Your grandmother was always a short, tubby woman," he explains, as if she is completely unknown to me — as in fact in many ways she is: "a woman full of sorrows, who didn't speak English, not a fancy mother." His father, he says, was his hero, an outdoorsman, and quite a learned man. My uncle is unsure of his facts, as he is of the propriety of his feelings, but he sketches in the first family map I've had of my grandmother's territory.

"They both came from Bobruisk in Belarus," he tells me. "Harry, the eldest in a family of six other brothers and a sister, had a father who spent all of his time studying in a *shul* while his sons worked a farm and served their turns in the Russian army. My father came to loath everything associated with Russia — the Czar, the anti-Semitism, the poverty, later the socialism and communism. My mother came from what she considered a higher social environment. She was the only daughter in the second or third marriage of a merchant, and with that difference always considered herself above Harry. He courted her at home, but he didn't get very far until he'd gone off to Canada and was writing what my mother used to call his 'lying letters' about the wonderful 'clean country' he'd discovered, urging her to join him."

"Harry was persuasive," my uncle says, and Sarah came, after all, to join him while he worked first on a kind of utopian farm of some Russian Jews — winter-time farmers he called them, who in winter would gather round the fire to read and talk politics, but who would disappear when the time came for planting in the spring. "That farm was so far from a rail-head," my uncle remembers my grandfather saying, "that in order to make it pay you'd have to grow gold."

"He loved the outdoors," my uncle continues, and it was the great irony of his life to spend so much of it in New York, and to die there. After the farm, he got another job in Canada working with his hands, laying track. "Pop used to say," my uncle adds, "that he was the only Jewish layer of track in Eastern Canada. He wouldn't take credit for being the only Jew to do that in all of Canada, though. 'What do I know about what goes on in Manitoba,' he'd say." For a few years after, he followed that track to the end of the line, and would get off with his dogs to spend months in the bush, buying furs from the Indians. "He was competition for the great Hudson Bay Company," my uncle says with a laugh, and while he loved it, shipping the furs to his brother who lived in Toronto, it was financial death. "His brother got rich, my father got poor," my uncle tells me, and my grandmother, a tough minded woman, pushed the family toward the Bronx while she pulled my grandfather out of his romance with the wilderness. But even then, the progress in New York was always northward toward more open spaces. "The mission was to get up to the northern Bronx," my uncle says, "where there was thought to be fresh air. My mother was mad for fresh air: '*hab a bissel luft* — grab some fresh air,' she'd always say. Life was built around fresh air."

"I always just took it for granted that she came here," my uncle shakes his head a little as if amazed now to contemplate it. "But here was this girl, leaving her father, leaving everything, packing up her bundles, and going to Canada. Canada! What did she know about Canada? Nothing. I mean she had the guts of a pirate to get on that damn ship, to pack up, to take Harry's money for the passage."

Years later, he explains, when he was married and was moving from the Village to midtown, he called her in the Bronx and said he wanted her to see the new apartment. He'd come to get her. But she wouldn't have it. "Sonny," she'd said to him, "if I could get from Bobruisk in Russia, to Sault St. Marie in West Algoma County, the Province of Ontario, in Canada, I can find 86th Street." And when he thought about it later, he tells me, "she *did* find it. She got, not to New York, where there would be others, Jews, around her, but to West Algoma County, and she found the apartment on 86th Street, too."

As my uncle says, she was a long way from "give me your tired, your hungry, your poor." No "huddled mass" there, "yearning to breathe free." But what was she yearning for, my uncle's pirate queen of a mother? And was my grandfather, her pirate king, sharing her great adventure?

Inseparable From Death

"After the first death, there is no other," Dylan Thomas once wrote; and for Sarah, after the death of her first child, there was nothing but the death of hope. Increasingly isolated in her determined grief, fed by the later deaths of Harry and so many children, she lived with ghosts and shadows.

"I don't remember grandma ever being happy," my uncle says. "My relationship with her was inseparable from death — we were moving from one death to another. I thought we'd never emerge." And as he talks, it's clear that, in fact, he hasn't. While my uncle's work as a journalist has compelled him to witness and record history shaped by human monsters who have served up carnage as never before, his understanding of death is familial. "We were bound together only by tragedy," he continues, explaining in a sentence what lies at the heart of all my grandmother's relationships.

"An incident occurred that changed my attitude toward her forever," my uncle tells me. "We were living in the Amalgamated Housing Project Apartments, down below Jerome Avenue. My sister was dying in the apartment. She was a kind of frail woman, the angel in the family, really. She had pneumonia, and was in an oxygen tent. One night — I don't know how long this had gone on — my father was in the kitchen, we were all awake, and he was reading when my mother came in screaming at him that his daughter was dying and he was sitting there reading a book. What did he mean by it? I can never forget how he looked up with his sweet face, stumped, ashamed; he couldn't believe it. A terrible woman, I remember thinking, but I couldn't find the words. I realized later that she was full of death, that she was just trying to say to her husband, basically, help me, be with *me*."

My uncle makes clear that from his child's eye view, now grown into firm adult conviction, my grandmother never did say it, to her husband or to anyone else in her family. That was her courage, and her madness. Or if she did find voice for her feeling, it was so hidden and protected by rage that my grandfather couldn't possibly hear it, nor could the others. When he died soon after, my grandmother was lost, finally and fatally, as dead in her life as if she had caught pneumonia herself, or one of the cancers that ravaged her children, or had fallen from a killing height to the streets below.

How to Perform a Funeral

The summer my grandmother was killed by a careless driver under the tracks of the El at the corner of Gun Hill Road and Jerome Avenue, I was home from college, working as a "Summer Playground Instructor" at P.S. 95 a few blocks away. The money was good, the work was easy — in short, I had nothing to complain of. Except that my walk to work and back took me right past my grandmother's favorite sitting bench. By 8:30 a.m. on most summer days, my grandmother would walk slowly up past the *shul*, turn right at the candy store, make her way along Gun Hill Road, then across Jerome, often jay walking on a diagonal under the El, to park herself on one of the wood and stone benches that backed onto Mosholu golf course, and fronted the busy stores of the neighborhood. People on their way to the train would pass her; so would students shuffling toward Dewitt Clinton H.S., shoppers at the A&P, dog walkers, moms with toddlers. My grandmother and a few bench-sharing companions were firmly planted for the parade. By mid-morning they had cleared out, though always to return by 4 p.m. when the human ramble rewound itself.

I passed my grandmother everyday that summer. If I was early, she was early; if I stayed late, she sat late. I was ashamed for wanting it, but I hoped that some mornings or afternoons I'd find her bench empty — not seriously empty, not terminally empty, but momentarily empty.

"Sonny," she'd say day-in, day-out, "why don't you visit me?" Or "Sonny, come up tonight for *gefilteh* fish." "Sonny, how's your sister? She never writes me." "Sonny, don't you know your grandmother any more?" Her greetings were invariably accompanied by stern looks and a chorus of resonant, disapproving clucks from her nattering companions who, I was sure, would spend most of the morning dissecting my ingratitude. It's not that I never visited, but I couldn't bring myself to stop by more than once a month, despite our proximity to each other. Always she plumbed the depths of the past for family slights and crimes to punish. The frustrations and malice that fueled her fantasies were uncontrolled. Once she told me that my father had been sniffing around other women while my dying mother was in the hospital. She said she'd told my mother about it while she was recovering from an operation that had removed her leg to the hip; she'd told my stepmother about it after she and my father married; and now she was telling me. An absurd accusation, presumably concocted to explain why my father — oppressed by his young wife's terminal illness and running between two jobs and child care — had occasionally been late for a hospital visit. It was a repellent act of pure desperation, the nastiest response to loss I could imagine, reenacted now nearly twenty years later as if time had no motion. All three of my parents had somehow managed to forgive my grandmother's malevolent nuttiness. I couldn't.

Though I'd been aware of my grandmother's stolid presence, like some rocky outcrop I had to negotiate on my daily voyaging, I didn't notice at all when she vanished from her post. She had wandered off course herself that morning, drifting away from the traffic light and the street corner to be hit from the side by a fast moving Plymouth, whose huge tail fins and toothy front grill must have made it seem for a moment like some dangerous sea creature. Tossed many feet, she'd broken up like a child's toy, dying later in Montefiore Hospital just a half mile away. My father told me about it, and about the funeral services to be held in Queens, a borough that was as familiar to me as Bobruisk.

I remember the day of my grandmother's burial only in bits and pieces. Though I wanted to get it right — perhaps since I felt I'd gotten so much else wrong in my unresponsive attention to her for years — my day was filled with miscues.

Putting on my only suit, a baggy brown wool blend that had no business being out of my closet in high summer, I stepped onto the IRT in the far northern reaches of the Bronx, with what seemed like enough time to launch an expedition in search of Mr. Livingston, or some other wanderer who might be lost on the outer edges of the known world. Somewhere in the belly of lower Manhattan, though, I had to change for a train east toward the land of cemeteries; and there, hanging one-handed onto the strap holder while trying, like a tourist, to read the map of totally unfamiliar names, I discovered myself spinning through dark tunnels farther and farther from my Grandmother's mortuary. "Shit," I kept thinking, slapping my hand with rhythmic agitation on my thigh, "shit, I'm on the wrong train. I'm going to be too late. I'll have to make an entrance; everybody will be watching me — the graceless, ungrateful grandson. She'll be buried by the time I get there. Where the hell am I? I'll have to get out to the cemetery by myself. Where *is* the cemetery?"

By the time I recovered my direction, I had my jacket bunched under my arm. Trying to pull my starched white shirt away from my clammy skin, I had also started to pull it out of my pants. I was pacing near the main doors of the train car, as if by moving quickly back and forth across that small area I could hurry the train toward my grandmother's body. I was half an hour late, and I had come undone.

But the dead, of course, will wait. Funeral services, I discovered after running four blocks from the subway station, have their own leisurely pace — though within the limits of good business sense. Things had just gotten started, and I was ushered, sweating and bedraggled, into the section reserved for family — though why there was need for separation with so small a group as my grandmother had assembled was perplexing. Beyond immediate family, attendance was thin. A few, like my father, were, I suppose, defined as "not quite so immediate family"; and there were some who had come as friends of the family. The rabbi who hadn't the slightest idea who my grandmother was, was saying wonderful things about her — formulaic musings mixed with family facts from a cheat sheet that my aunt and uncle had provided for the occasion. Loving and beloved was the message, brave and protective, resilient and remarkable. I had no idea why it wasn't left to my uncle and aunt to eulogize my grandmother; after all, these were just their own messages gathered and thrown back at them by a stranger. But the protocol was clear, and weighed down for the first time in years with a *yarmulke* atop my thick hair, I joined the rest of the family, nodding in prayer-like agreement with the Reb's anemic insights into the life of a woman who had eluded us all.

Having been identified several times that day as belonging to a specific community — one of the group that sprang from Sarah's needs, desires, energies, I was surprised to discover as we gathered for our limo ride to the cemetery that I'd never felt more aware of my separateness. When the family lined up like dignitaries to thank guests for coming, I found myself shaking hands with my father, as if I was part of a special society from which he was excluded. I couldn't think of another time in which we had been together somewhere but had not been identified with each other. I felt like an impostor among impostors, and when my father explained that he was headed back to Brooklyn to finish his day's work, I wanted desperately to go with him.

The drive to the graveyard was marked by the level drone of commonplace conversations — my cousins and I talking the talk of bored teens, awkward with the occasion and our presence at it. At the same time, a lugubrious pathos hung over the event, measured in the dark-suited dignity of the professionally mournful drivers and other functionaries of the funeral home. My grandmother would have liked being at the heart of the matter, and no doubt would have relished the drama and attention. But mostly, I think, she'd have recognized the lack of sincerity that to an extent clouded the proceedings, offering up one last cause for complaint — a kind of final "I told you so" to decry this unsatisfactorily and unrealistically soft ending to her relentlessly, often willfully, hard life.

In one of his wonderfully clear and human poems William Carlos Williams proclaims that he "will teach [us] ... / how to perform a funeral." Having reminded us that a life of value requires a death with dignity, he comes at last to the essential lines: "sit openly — / to the weather as to grief." On the day of my grandmother's funeral I was filled with anxiety, frustration, and sadness; and I was simply incapable of "sitting openly as to grief." More than thirty years later, still puzzled by the facts and features of my grandmother's life and death, I grieve for her at last — for her energy scattered by sorrow, for her delight diminished by fear, for her love hardened by solitude. I grieve her world of lost connections, and my incapacity to comprehend the force of her need for my time, my affection — however tried and tested, my sympathy.

VI.

BE HAPPY

What Do You Mean?

No one in our family knows what the last words of my step-grandmother Yetta were. She died sitting up in bed, fully clothed save for one shoe which had partly slipped off and was dangling. She was waiting in an empty house for my mother and father to return from Kennedy Airport, where they had gone to meet a flight of incoming relatives. But the words which stick in my mind as her final say — though she spoke on for years in my presence — were her inquisitorial demands that my grandfather explain himself.

"What do you mean?" she snapped at him. "What do you *meeee-un*?" she hissed, stretching it. What do you MEAN?" she exclaimed with emphasis.

I heard her unload the question repeatedly, a year or so before my grandfather died, while my mother, father, and I were driving out into the country to deliver my grandparents to Unity House, a vacation resort of the International Ladies Garment Workers Union. Here, I supposed, they would spend the next two weeks uncovering a "unity" that was invisible in their non-resort territory back in the Bronx.

The harsh refrain which she pulled out and flashed readily, like a cranky calling card, had behind it the discontents of a lifetime of confronting her husband's unrealistic schemes for an improved quality of life. I had rarely heard an adult use that dismissive tone to another, and I was embarrassed for both my embattled grandfather and my attacking grandmother. But he absorbed all with an equanimity that suggested years of such skirmishing. I have no memory of what the precise question of meaning was about that afternoon. But the issue seemed larger than could be contained in the back seat of my Dad's old Ford Fairlane. "What do you mean," she might have been saying, "by failing to provide decently for your family?" Or, "what do you mean by bringing me to live in one slum after another?" "What do you mean by dreaming away our pittance on get rich schemes?" "What do you mean by our life together?"

Clinging

"My mother seemed happy in her marriage," my mother tells me, surprisingly. "But there was some lack there. There wasn't a hot romance. I never saw them hug or kiss. But he referred to her as his princess, and she cooked him his favorites — *borsht* and pickled herring, *latkes*, *flanken*, and kept him neatly pressed and shined, ready for any opportunity that might arise. You might say they were clinging together." But in the embrace, Yetta's sharp edges of frustration were never fully sheathed and could draw blood, and Simon's enveloping, easy going calm could be suffocating.

By the day of my wedding, my grandmother Yetta was barely a shell of her former self. Hunched by bone loss and angina pain, with her swollen and distended aorta pulsing visibly in her abdomen, she looked every bit of her eighty years. She had been ill for decades, but alone only for five years, since the death of her husband. Simon, a tall, ruddy man from a village near Minsk that sounded very much like "Dogshitz" when he said it — a source of much amusement when I was ten years old — had come to New York where, with an army of other Russian Jews, he was working as a machine operator in the garment district's sweatshops. He met my grandmother when he visited his sister and mother who were living in the "real" America of Syracuse, New York. She was on the tall side, and slender, my mother tells me, the new world way my grandfather liked his women, rather than Slavic squat, and heavy.

Young Simon spoke Yiddish, almost exclusively; Yetta, despite her ethnic name, spoke only English. It couldn't have been a promising start, but both were needy and ready. Simon's boyish loneliness must have been appealing in a way that announced a man needing to be cared for. And Yetta was a bona fide established caretaker, seeing to the needs of a father who at the age of twenty-nine had lost a fortune when his cigar factory went up in smoke — and his sight, it is said, in the shock that followed.

My grandmother's family had lived an American success story. But they had also inhabited an American tragedy which brought the progress of their horse and buggy to a halt, closed the big house, disbanded the servants, and compelled my great grandmother, still a young mother of seven, to open a small grocery store for day to day survival. My grandmother became her father's window onto the world, his eyes, his hope. He became her cage and her promise, limiting yet defining her. He would sit, she would read to him. He would listen, she would play the piano for him. He would walk, she would guide him, holding fast to his arm. When she married, he fainted, unable to face his isolating darkness without her. When she left, he was frantic, and not to be consoled.

I can only wonder at what my grandmother expected when she allowed herself to be taken off to the tenements of lower Manhattan, a long way from the grassy front yards of upstate, and even farther from her comfortable role as essential daughter at the center of her family, however seriously damaged that family may have been. Did she envision the isolation of being Simon's prized trophy American, foreign to all the foreigners that now made up her community? Could she foresee that Simon would make no money operating cutting machines for coat makers? Or that while he was teaching himself English in these new *shtetls* of the city — stubbornly trekking through *The New York Times* every day — she, speaking only English in a Yiddish neighborhood, would be without meaningful language in her own country? Could she comprehend the concrete landscape? The lack of privacy? The loneliness amidst crowds of people?

What she found, my mother tells me, was nearly complete isolation and absence of purpose until her first child, my uncle Harry, was born. With a son to mind, and then a daughter, she was the family conscience keeper, guardian of hearth and home. Absorbed by the hope and promise of her male child, and watchful of his younger sister, she was sometimes tolerant of her childlike husband's repeated economic flights of fancy, and sometimes found them intolerable. In the full flower of her matriarchy, she was protective, praiseworthy, yet aggravating, frustrated and frustrating, hapless and shrill, all the while waiting for her son to do what the father could not — make the family proud.

In the Tombs

"There were lots of days my father didn't work," my mother says after supper one night. I've lugged a fairly large portable tape recorder west with me from New York so she can tell me more about her parents; and though she seems uneasy about remembering them into a microphone, she clearly wants to get this "family business" part of my visit over with. Staunchly determined to please me, she plunges in.

"During the slow season," she says, the men would go down to the shop — to play cards, to find out if there was any work, just to be there. You didn't hang around home if you could help it. It wasn't manly, and besides, you were sure to be in the way."

"So grandma encouraged grandpa to futz away his time with guy talk? Weren't there responsibilities to take care of closer to home?" I ask, flashing my right-thinking, sensitive-new-age-man aura.

"Well, it was good for his spirit," my mother says, "and good for grandma's too, to have the house cleared of reminders of failure. And besides, it was always possible that something would happen downtown, but you had to be there to take advantage of it. He used to say 'you had to watch yourself as if a fire might threaten you: *hit zich vi fun a feier!*' Be alert." Which was hugely comic, considering how little Simon really watched out for himself, or seemed to care about being taken unawares.

As far as family lore goes, getting arrested was the only thing my grandfather accomplished from days down at the shop waiting for a sniff of work. "I'm going, just to find out," he said, hopping the #6 train for a fifty minute ride downtown. He wasn't heard from again that day or night.

While my grandfather didn't play cards, he did like to talk, and talking always went best with a good cigar. In fact, he was puffing away happily, schmoozing with his "*lantsleit,*" his pals, more or less from the old country, smack under the prominent "No Smoking" sign, when his great adventure began. My mother says simply, "along came a policeman," like "along came a spider," or, from the old rock song, "along came Jones." He must have been there to hassle the immigrants. After all, why walk up the flights of stairs when no problems had been reported, except to nose out violations? Hard though it is to believe, it was a smoker's raid, and they took my grandfather, swept up like a dust ball, to the Tombs.

The name conjures The Night of the Living Dead, blood, gore, torment. But for my congenial grandfather, it was a moment to be savored. When it got near the witching hour and my grandfather hadn't come home, my grandmother called his boss to find out if he knew where Simon was. My grandfather wasn't the sort of man to just disappear without notice; he was, after all, a family man, and responsible after a fashion. His only other encounter with the law had come when he was asked to describe a thief who had been working the subways, and, who, thinking he could lift a nice bottle of scotch, had been caught trying to take from my grandfather's coat pocket a pint bottle of urine that was on its way to a medical lab.

My poor grandmother was told her husband had been jailed, but not why. It seems the judge had said that my grandfather could either pay a fine or be locked up, and, having no money, he'd opted for free overnight accommodations. My mother supposes he could have found a way to call; there was no phone in the apartment, but there was one down the hall where a message could be left. But he was probably having too much fun to think about it.

When my grandmother met him early the next morning, both sleepy children in tow, my grandfather came up from the bowels of Manhattan's most serious prison smiling and chattering, as if had been away for a country weekend.

"Darling," he'd said to my grandmother in a voice lively with wonder and delight — "*kinderlech*," he'd said to my mother and her brother, as if starting to tell some marvelous fairy tale — "I met some really nice people here, wonderful people. And they brought food in, and we talked all night about everything. But the most amazing thing was that sitting next to me was someone from Russia, a Count, and I'm sure I remembered him. Though of course he didn't know me. But there we were together, sharing salami, me and the Count, talking like brothers. Back home he wouldn't even see me to spit on me. But here... We live in a wonderful country that can bring a poor man and royalty together."

Be Happy

I suppose you could call my grandfather Simon a *luftmensch*, literally an air man, a guy with his head in the clouds, though I don't know if you'd ever have done that to his face. He had a serious notion of himself, but like Sholom Aleichem's Menachem Mendel he was forever luckless and dreaming. "Be *frailech*," was his favorite line to his kids: "be happy." But how?

My mother tells me that when he was young, Simon was dapper. "There was a painting of him," she says, "a touched up photo, really, that showed him with lovely black hair that had a curl to it. And he was very well dressed in a nice dark suit, with a honey yellow chain and watch dangling down the front of a silky vest. He was very proud of that painting and hung it in the house for years."

"My father had very good taste in clothes," she continues. "Better than my mother. Her clothes, when she was young, were made in Syracuse by a nun, and she had no ideas about dressing. But my father knew what he liked and what he wanted, and he would take my mother downtown and would pick out her dresses on the occasions when a new dress was called for, like for a wedding or bar mitzvah."

But all his good taste didn't matter much if he couldn't afford the good things, or, generally, even the ordinary ones, in life. Which was the circumstance in which he usually found himself. "My father tried so hard to get out of the shops," my mother remembers. "But he always bounced back."

"One day," she says, smiling at the memory, "he came home with a great big thing like a pot to put on the stove and stir. It had little faucets on the bottom. He had decided that he was going to make perfume. He didn't know anything about the process. He didn't realize that for perfume to retain its odor you needed ambergris. He didn't use anything, just tried to boil down the flowers somehow, and the residue perfume lost whatever smell it had right away. Even at that, he used a forest of flowers to make a thimble of scent. The fancy pot which you couldn't even cook chicken in was a total loss. I don't think he managed to bottle a single vial of perfume. It was typical."

"He saw money possibilities everywhere," my mother continues, "but he wasn't able to convert promising ideas into anything even close to practical realities. What he lacked going in was money, and so what he missed going out was money. One of his best failed ideas was to put umbrellas in shoeshine shops, so that if you were caught in a sudden downpour you could pick one up and return it to a different location when the rain stopped. What he didn't think through, was that you needed thousands of umbrellas to make it work. I don't think that he ever had enough stock to try the plan out. Grandma seemed very nice about it, though. Maybe she was as unrealistic as he was.

"For a while he was a kind of mobile pawnbroker,

going around to the different shops with a beautiful tiny scale he'd bought for himself so that he could buy gold from the workers."

"What kind of gold would they have?" I ask.

"Maybe watches," my mother speculates, "maybe rings, maybe buttons, who knows, maybe even fillings. It depends on how desperate they might be. But the scales cost more than any gold he weighed on them."

"Then," my mother explains, "Grandpa decided to go from buyer to seller. He thought he could be a traveling salesman. He couldn't sell *anything*. Salesmen have to be a little on the — I don't know — they have to be good bullshitters. Grandpa just wasn't — not because he didn't want to be, but he just couldn't bring it off. He went out and bought a car, a Ford open car, like a touring car. He was not a good driver, though. When he saw something coming, instead of turning away from it, my father would put out his hand, as if he was going to push the thing away, whether it was another car, a horse and buggy, or a person. But even if he could have gotten to someplace he wanted to go, he just couldn't sell. He was going to put men's clothes in the car and sell them to the men who worked on farms in the northeast. That was his plan. And why not? His brother-in-law, Max, had done it, and had made money at it. But grandpa never earned a dime by it. He only had the car a year."

I can picture Simon driving up through the smell of cow manure, climbing out into the muck of the farmyard to hawk heavy black trousers to dour men who mistrusted his foreignness, his Jewishness. I wonder what words he could possibly have used to reach them, this man from Minsk and the Bronx. While my mother is talking, I try to remember Charley's requiem speech for Willy Loman in *Death of a Salesman*: "Nobody dast blame this man. You don't understand: Willy was a salesman. And for a salesman, there is no rock bottom to the life... He's a man way out there in the blue, riding on a smile and a shoeshine. And when they start not smiling back — that's an earthquake... Nobody dast blame this man. A salesman is got to dream, boy. It comes with the territory." But for Simon, salesman wanna-be, reluctant patriarch, the "dream" was the *only* territory.

For Yetta, swept along in the aimless flow of my grandfather's feckless yearnings, the cost was great. With her own dreams diminished or unspoken, she could offer at the end only a sad picture of confused loneliness and a lifetime's habit of carping and coping. "Still," my mother says, "she was a survivor. It was her one true gift to her children and grandchildren."

VII.

TWO MOTHER LOVE
(ELIZABETH AND ANN)

Baggage

Yesterday at lunch, an old friend of mine refused to be teased by her salad-eating table mates as she tucked into a thick piece of death by chocolate layer cake. "You *can't* make me feel guilty," she said, "I'm Italian. My mother's done it all. Momma Mia! If I ate, if I didn't; if I kept company with boys, if I didn't; if I studied, and if I only pretended to. She talked endlessly about diets, but kept the pasta piled high; and when I finally dieted, she told me I'd stunt my growth and damage any children I might have if I didn't stop this foolishness and eat. If I walked home with a guy, she'd let me know what one thing they wanted from me. And if I didn't have a boyfriend, she'd ask if I wanted to be an old maid all my life. When I came home with an A in something besides Home Economics she'd smile with pride, but remind me that reading led to glasses, and glasses led to loneliness. Faced with the shambles of my usual report card of C's, D's, she'd go through her full series of 'I give up' shrugs and twitches to let me know that she had tried and it was clear that I was a nowhere girl whose life would be wasted. Chocolate cake? *Oh please*. Don't waste your breath."

A series of "oh yeahs" circled the table from both women and men. A parade of moms were conjured, all proud and complaining, all burned deep into their adult children's psyches. As it happens, the way we'd gone from cake to mother memory, without so much as a gesture toward a proper segue, didn't surprise me at all. I'd been thinking about mothers pretty steadily for weeks, trying to figure out what to say about this essential woman in my family, more intimidating to write about than my grandmothers because better known and much more loved. Write about the women, my wife had said. Of course. But how? The cartoony conscience keeper was a good image for lunchtime amusement, but we all knew that it was just a coping mechanism to get distance on the complex, often unsettling confusions of a relationship that remained crucial and misunderstood. As I headed back to work, I found myself humming old tunes, repeating nursery rhymes, remembering mom-laden schoolyard taunts, mothers on my mind: "How I recall my dear old mother, putting me to bed; she tucked me in and to her sleepyhead she said... Hey, momma's boy... Yo Momma!... Yuh muthuh wears army boots... Muthafucka... Throw Momma from the train, a kiss... I want a girl just like the girl that married dear old dad... Holy Mary, mother of God, pray for us sinners now." Revered and reviled, judging and judged, guardian of our comings and goings, now and, it seems, forever: how, I wonder, can one ever hope to unpack so much baggage?

Names

"I'll need some memorable names," the bank clerk in the Yorkshire city where I'm living says when I come in to open my new account. "It's just for identification purposes." She wants my mother's maiden name for starters, and there's the rub. I've tripped on this before — calling Visa's customer service number or my long distance phone carrier, anywhere that wants to protect my credit from the unscrupulous who'd steal my secrets. "Which mother?" I want to say, as if to confess an intimate family detail — that I've had two of them. Or, having forgotten which mother's name I first presented, I'll confidently offer up my mother's maiden name like a secret handshake, only to be told by a skeptical voice at the other end that that's not the name they've been given. "Oh," I'll say, trying to sound aw-shucks-gee-whiz innocent, "you must mean my stepmother's maiden name; I couldn't remember which one I wrote down." I always feel somehow "guilty" when this happens, as if they've understood my true criminal intent, or I've been caught with my hand in the till.

I'm not sure why I've ever given my birth mother's name when asked by some authority figure for an identity code word. I've not lived with her, been cared for by her, heard, seen, smelled, touched her at any time in the life I can remember. Yet I respond like I'm a smarty pants schoolboy facing a trick question in a spelling bee or a game of twenty questions, and I mustn't be fooled if I want to please authority and get it "right." I'm not usually a literalist, but, awkwardly, I often seem unable to get past the received notion that a "mother" is a person who literally gives life — a "source," so that I can act instead on my obvious intuitive and practical knowing that the mother who has raised you is the mother you've got. And mine, having arrived in our family not long after I learned to walk and talk, has been generous, supportive, unequivocally loving for virtually all of the five-plus decades of my life. Yet while day to day I haven't thought much about the other woman over the years, she's still there too, a name and a shadowy presence that I share with bankers, lawyers, customer-service reps, who know her almost as well as I do.

Voices

Dead before I was three, she is only pictures and stories to me. The photos that are turning from brown to blanched yellow show a small woman, dark hair in a sporty boyish cut, with a straight-at-you stare that's softened ever so slightly by the faintest of smiles. Her gaze seems sad and serious. In the one I keep coming back to, she sits on a heavy floral print couch with her arm around her small son and daughter; it looks as if she may have just finished whispering something in their ears. Though I listen hard, the faded paper holds its silence. Other voices speak for her.

"She was fierce, angry, that's what I think I remember," my older sister tells me. "I mean, it was all a lifetime ago, and I was very small. I don't think she raised her voice, but she didn't just talk to me. She gave commands. She was severe."

"She was strong-willed," my father says. "She had energy to burn, and she had high principles. She took no guff, and she loved to argue. But never in a hurtful way."

"She was brave and generous," my uncle says. "My favorite sister. I always thought she was gorgeous, and very loving."

These three are the only people left who can be said to have known the woman they're conjuring for me, my birth mother, Elizabeth. But for each, and so for me, Elizabeth is a figure stuck in time, defined not so much by the person she had been as by the disease that destroyed her. Her last months are what my sister knows — her immense tiredness and fretfulness. They're the high wall of misery that my father needs to climb over to recapture his young wife. They offer the shape of an image fixed in my uncle's mind for more than half a century.

Words

"She gave me my first books," my uncle says, laughing. "She had bookcases in her bedroom, and she gave me the job of dusting those books, and of course I would sit and read them. When I couldn't put one down, she just gave it to me. I still have them all.

"Once I went to see your mother when she was in the hospital. She was terribly sick — she'd just had an amputation. I was twenty-four years old, working at the paper, going out with a beautiful woman from Arkansas; things couldn't have been better for me. This woman and I went in together for the visit, and there was my sister sitting up in bed and dressed up to greet me and to alleviate my own feeling of horror. It was a pretty short stay. We chatted, and she gave me a book of poems for a birthday present. When I got down to the street afterwards, I fainted dead away. It was the first and last time that ever happened."

He gets up from the sofa where we've been sitting and pulls a yellowed copy of John Donne's poems off a shelf nearby, opening it for me to a long inscription written in an unsteady hand. It's a lofty and effusive verse dedication, filled with delight and hyperbole, a kind of intensely personal bad writing that I'm a little embarrassed to be reading as I look for the woman that was my mother in it.

"Oh the exquisite marvel of a beautiful poem," she has written. "Words gliding in harmony,"

> Painting, singing, telling of the lives of men
> Of the little things that make their lives
> And the great that destroy.
> Lifting you on their gossamer
> Wings till you reach the sky,
> And mingling with the stars,
> Behold the wonders of infinity
> From their lofty heights.
> A poem — the voice of God
> Speaking through man.

So, she was a romantic, I say to myself with a bit of a wince and a smile, then the last lines catch my eye: "3/25/46 for 5/2/46. I love you very much, Lilla." My uncle stands looking at me, not speaking. He waits until I've made the connection in time, through time. What I'm looking at is my dying mother's careful gift offered more than a month early in full knowledge that she'd be dead before May — a message of connection that admits death's dark presence but denies its authority.

Talk

"Your mother came from a family of talkers; she had opinions about everything and she challenged everyone," my father says to me. "Politics, news, art, work, you name it, she had an idea about it.

The only times she was really at rest seemed to be when she had her nose in a book.

"She could go at it all day long with her sisters," he tells me when I press him. "It never seemed to be about anything that made sense to me. She never had harsh words for me, or for your sister, or you. But when her family sat down together, the girls fought about everything, from whose boss was most important, to whether the food was hot or cold, to whose house they'd meet at next."

"A couple of times," my father says with a laugh, "I thought she'd get me into real trouble. 'Just look at that,' she'd say when something that wasn't right caught her eye. Are you going to sit there? *Do something.*' Once when we were driving across country on our honeymoon, and I was still getting to know your mother, we stopped in Texas for lunch. It was an empty diner, except for a few locals having coffee. We studied the menu and ordered something like hash browns and onion and red pepper omelets — something with so much grease it would coat your teeth for days. I mean it wasn't classy dining, not the sort of place you'd want to be in unless you were passing through at mealtime. Before long we noticed this sign up near the register that said no Negroes could eat there; and even though it was probably doing blacks a favor to forbid them entry to that particular culinary hole, your mother was angry, very angry. 'They can't do that,' she said in a loud voice. 'We can't eat here, and we won't pay for this meal, either.' Pushing her plate away, and telling me to 'tell them,' she walked out. I was expected to follow as soon as I'd finished telling the diner owner where he could stuff his racially compromised omelets. 'Elizabeth,' I said in as much whisper as I could manage and still be heard. 'You can't do that. Don't you know where we are?' She never turned around, never looked back, never stopped in her steady march out the door. And she never asked me what I'd said. She just waited in the car while I went up to the counter. In fact, I didn't say a word, just paid the guy quickly before they could get up a lynch mob to see about these uppity northerners. Jews no less. You had to admire her principles and her feistiness, but often it just felt like I was being swept up into some kind of game of will, whether I wanted to play or not."

That's Him

"That's him," she told my father, "that's him. He laughed at me and took my seat."

My father remembers that they were at Rockaway Beach, and she was pointing into a mob of about 30 guys who were gathered around someone sitting in a shady alcove and playing the guitar.

"I was sitting just over there," she says, "and when I got up to get a drink he threw my towel out and took my seat. Are you going to let him do that?"

"Well, what could I do?" my father asks with something between a smile and a grimace. "Thirty guys — I thought they'd kill me. I pushed into the crowd, just me in my bathing suit. The group parted to let me through. Moses and the Red Sea. 'Did you take this woman's place?' I asked. 'Did you throw her things out? What do you mean by it?'"

"'Not me,' he said, 'I never.'

"'Oh yes you did, you bully you,' Elizabeth was shouting behind me. The crowd vanished, leaving the guy alone with us.

"'Go on, go on, tell him,' she said. 'He can't get away with that.' He'd picked up his guitar by now and was moving away, in full retreat. Elizabeth had the field and didn't seem ready to let go. She followed him, prodding me to go in front of her, calling out her continuing outrage over my shoulder. Afterwards, face flushed with righteous triumph, she took up her spot, pulled open her book, and was instantly lost to the world."

Picturing her contemplative calm while her displaced enemy wandered the boardwalk looking again for a place to impress his pals, I wondered who this fierce woman with a bookish bent might be. Soon after, she needed every nerve-twitch of force and fight; cancer pushed her out of all her safe places without even a hint of apology.

"It all happened so fast, just after you were born,"

my father says. "It cost me my friendship with my cousin, Sol, who was our doctor. I suppose it was stupid of me, but I blamed him for not recognizing the melanoma on the back of her leg. And even though Sol and I had grown up together, I wouldn't speak with him after she died. For more than fifty years — until last year, in fact, when we both apologized to each other. Neither of us have long, and we didn't want this stupid thing to go with us, wherever it is we may be going."

"I was floored," my father says. "It seemed like a death sentence that came only minutes after she'd been perfectly healthy. First the terrible fatigue; then the diagnosis from a specialist we'd decided to see about why she could barely hold her head up. One of her sisters was already dead from some kind of cancer, and one from pneumonia. We knew death; knew enough to be afraid; knew enough to know that fear was pointless."

"She was in and out of the hospital for a year," my father tells me. "I was up to my eyeballs in medical bills. I couldn't even afford the subway. At the end of the month I'd have to walk to work from our place way up near the end of the Woodlawn-Jerome line to my school near Yankee Stadium — sometimes even down to mid-town for a meeting. She was so sick all the time, in such pain. And then she was gone."

My father says it like it was the shutting off of a light bulb, where the darkness is sudden and complete. He won't talk any more about it, about her, and no amount of coaxing will get him to throw that light switch back on. I can read about melanoma. I can try to envision his hurt and solitude, his frantic busyness with the two children to care for. I can hear him describe the meals he'd cook, the bedtime stories he'd read, the weekends at the playground. I can envision hospital visits, and homecomings to a cold flat where he was the only adult presence. But I can't get him to revisit any further the year of my mother's long dying, the year of my sister's confused childhood and my own infancy. The shadows of Elizabeth's terribly short life seem suddenly longer, darker now than ever before, wrapping my father, and so our family's collective memory, in an ever-tighter shroud.

Apologize

"I can only really remember one event with mother," my sister tells me, "and that's too bad because it's not a good one. I was about four years old, and I must have done something wrong, though I don't have any idea now of what it could have been. Pop was cast as the heavy; his assignment was to discipline me until I apologized to mother for whatever it was I did. And being confused or stubborn or angry, I steadfastly refused. Pop would spank me half-heartedly then bring me out into mother's presence and she'd ask if I was ready to apologize. I wasn't; I probably didn't even know what the word meant. So I was taken back out of her presence and a few minutes later brought back again with the same results. I don't remember, really, how long it went on, or if I did apologize finally, or if the energy just wore out.

"What I do remember is mother's unforgiving face and voice, her insistence that I confess. She may have been wonderful, and this was probably an event of no importance. But it's what I think of when I think of her. She must have been so unhappy."

Continuity

When my oldest son was born I found myself wishing that Elizabeth had been alive to share the moment. While I had not often thought of her from year to year, the prospect of my own parenting made me want to have my family complete. I tried to picture the two paternal grandmothers gathered round the boy's crib, each looking down, proud and approving. But while my stepmother Ann was in full motion and voice, holding Peter against her face, cooing about how he was a pussycat, good enough to take a bite out of, delicious, then nibbling and nuzzling with her lips at his soft, soft face and neck — my birth mother, Elizabeth, was hanging back, still and voiceless. She looked on with longing and sadness, but didn't move, didn't reach out to caress or whisper sweetly. She was a watcher at the family feast, and always would remain so.

It seems terribly unjust that my birth mother died without leaving behind for me a proper remembered identity, an animated voice and image to conjure in daydreams about family continuity and continuance. I love the idea of my mother, as my mother must have loved the idea of the child she would not live to see grow into manhood. But perhaps, after all, there can only be one mother for a child, and my stepmother Ann, substance not shadow, filled that space in the family.

She Will Bring Her Piano

Apparently there were no bumpy beginnings. "Will she bring her piano?" was all my sister asked when my father sat down to explain the coming of a new mother in our Bronx apartment. I can't recall any doubts of my own, just a powerful desire for attention and affection. We had been motherless for about two years at the time, cared for occasionally by a nanny, and by my father's unceasing watchfulness. He would hurry home from his days in the classroom, relieve and release Fanny, our caretaker, cook his specialty scrambled eggs or matzo brie, bathe us, read to us, even sing to us in a deep baritone from the *Fireside Book of Folksongs*. Sometimes he'd end the day with a chorus of the bouncy "Froggy Went a Courtin'," though increasingly he'd offer up the achingly painful "When Israel was in Egypt land, let my people go," or a lovely lamentation about the hard life of

"Nicodemus the slave." Despite his best efforts, the sadness was palpable.

On weekends he'd take us off to parades, puppet shows, or children's plays, whisking us away if he thought there were too many sniffling, coughing people in the audience because he couldn't afford to have us sick. In the summertime, we'd all slip out of the city to spend our time in some Adirondack Camp with an Indian name, where my father was Head Counselor, and where my sister was a junior camper, and where I would sit at the waterfront with various teenage kids who'd care for me in a kind of rotation. That's where I first met my mother-to-be who, as things got serious with my dad, must have sacrificed her scant vacation to trek north from the city to test for herself and for us the unpredictable and perhaps dangerous waters of parenthood.

That summer, I'm told, my sister was a happy camper, but I was sick for weeks with bronchitis. I must have seemed a scrawny, frightened, fretful kid, no easy assignment for a woman who had still to convince herself that her relationship with my father was right, let alone that she'd be glad of her role as surrogate mother. But she says that she discovered early-on that I loved to sit in the camp's old station wagon, hour after hour, pretending to drive, or just breathing in the smells of leather, wood, and oil. Or that I could be happy lying on my bed next to her while she read her book out loud.

"Read to me Ann Miller," she says was my constant demand. "But you won't understand this, sweetheart." "Read to me Ann Miller." So she read her Shakespeare, and I was appeased and content, happy in her presence and somehow pleased with the lush rhythms of the Bard's tragic tales.

That's how we got to know each other, so that when autumn came round at last, I was an easy convert. The much desired piano arrived as expected, offering me a playground on which to push my bull dozer, or spread out my toy soldiers, or even just sit my teddy bear where I could watch him and he could observe my games. A vintage Steinway upright, appropriate for a small apartment, it presented a world in itself, with cliffs and plains, vistas, places to play hide and seek, mysterious workings of machinery where hammers and strings came together to form a hazard through which my action figures could dash and duck, Flash Gordon-like, in pursuit of evil doers. Sometimes the Steinway became a life size prop in my fantasy enactments of adventure stories, as I ran around the room challenging bad guys for the good of the world, sliding out from behind the spindly legs of the stool to confront men in black with evil grins and goals.

For my sister, old enough to know the proper uses of a piano, it was at first thrills, then torments, as she embarked on music lessons with my new mother's own piano teacher, the wonderful, redoubtable, indomitably stern and idealistic Mabel, who didn't see a child, but a repository to fill with information and discipline.

I would often accompany my sister on lesson day, sitting at the kitchen table, playing with my little soldiers and eating jello prepared for me by Mabel's mother, delighting in the attention while my sister shriveled before her attentive adults. Years later, she told my mother how much she hated those lessons, being in the spotlight with no playfulness or humor in the situation. "Strike from the shoulder, not from the hands," was the battle-cry she remembered, and though she'd wanted to strike out in all sorts of directions, she'd simply tried helplessly to efface herself before the harsh landscape of gleaming white and black keys. My mother had no idea.

Still, the piano bond between mother and daughter has been firm through the years, the delight of the first promise impossible to shatter even with the punishment of learning to play. And long after that piano had been sold to raise money for college tuitions, and then been replaced by a smaller, lesser instrument in a small California retirement home, my mother's piano embodied all the potent anxious hope and love of those first months together. Taking me aside to explain the secret that has been no secret for decades, my mother hopes I'll understand that she's planning to leave her latest piano to my sister and has written it down in her will. I *do* understand, and my sister, who already has a large piano that she doesn't play, accepts with pure pleasure our mother's gift of love.

In the Kitchen

"Food's what won me," I tell my mother; "pasta is powerful."

My mother loves to cook, and I discovered that I love to eat — a match made in remarriage heaven. But for my mother, food was not just a way to my heart, it was the heart of the fortress that she built, the command center of family life, the reason for being in the kitchen, sanctum of sanctums.

I remember once hearing the novelist Paule Marshall describe how in her house the women were "poets in the kitchen." It was not just a work room, but a family gathering place, safe and warm, where "the women threw off the drab coats and hats, seated themselves at the large center table, drank their cups of tea or cocoa, and talked... freewheeling, wide-ranging, exuberant talk... And their talk was a refuge." But as far as I can tell, no one was ever allowed to cross the threshold of my mother's kitchen. Her kitchen was a place for efficiency and action, not storytelling — not a territory to be shared with friends or relatives. My mother's reasoning was always that her Bronx kitchen was a small place, and that too many cooks, or even pot watchers, would spoil any broth. It was clearly the place in the house where she was completely in charge and didn't have to talk or even listen much. Moving into and out of the kitchen, serving up meals, gathering dirty dishes even before people had a chance to finish eating, she was always dancing on the edges of family talk —moving in when it pleased her, or enjoying the silence that she hung like a curtain around her, claiming the necessity to be busy at the stove, sink, or fridge while others identified and solved the world's or the neighborhood's problems.

Last year when I visited in California it was still the same. Ignoring offers of help and a frustrated chorus of requests to please sit down, she spent the first part of each family meal piling more food on the table than anyone could possibly want or eat, and the second part clearing away the mountains of leftovers, packing them up for the freezer in ancient, much treasured Tupperware containers, and returning the kitchen to pristine condition. Piles of moist turkey and small hills of the leanest corned beef were cocooned in aluminum foil, wedged side by side with onion bagels, each silver overcoat scotch-taped with a penciled label against the possibility of some future misuse. Cereal boxes were dressed in plastic sleeping bags, rubber-banded at the top to preserve freshness then returned to the shelf to await the next encounter with milk, sugar, and bananas. Muffins, pound cakes, jams, veggie sausages, hard boiled eggs, mocha mix, jars of pickles, various rolls and breads, canisters of coffee beans from Trader Joe's, all found their distinct and protected spots in the fridge.

It wasn't about freshness, of course; it was about order. For my mother, it must have been a habit born of the necessity to manage a family living not so much in a big city but within a tight space. Our rent-controlled place in the shadow of busy Montefiore Hospital and park-like Woodlawn Cemetery was too good a deal to let go of. But it was squeezed for the four of us, and filled to overflow by the five we became when my mother's ill mother came to recover from surgery and stayed for ten years.

Frail and wasted, my grandmother was, nonetheless, a formidable presence planted in front of the TV in the central space of our living room, morning, afternoon, and evening, frequently querulous and demanding of her daughter. From the small, screen-protected portion of the living room that had become my working and sleeping space, I could hear her talking to the flickering figures of Jackie Gleason and Trixie, Lucy and Desi, Sid Caesar and his hapless crew. I could hear her laughter die into a persistent and painful cough, and knew my mother would be in to ease her into a less constricting sitting position, or to see that she held the nitroglycerin capsule under her tongue to soften the pain of her cramping heart. Often my grandmother would fall asleep in front of the set and would have to be wakened and escorted to the bathroom and then to bed in the back room that had once belonged to my mother and father, who now slept in a space partially partitioned off to accommodate my sister as well as their own bed and dresser. It was a bad, sad situation, with illness and death hovering in the crowded air, and few doors to shut against it; but there was no getting around it. Little wonder, then, at my mother's impenetrable kitchen stronghold, with all its spaces hidden from the rest of us, and its tools and products shrink-wrapped and neatly filed in manageable cold storage bins. But it was not freezer-bagged or cocooned love that was proffered in my mother's house. The food that was delivered out of that cooking hideaway was, like my mother's love for us all, warm when it needed warmth, hot when it needed heat, abundant and delicious.

My Brother's Cane

"It's *such* a pain in the neck — literally," my mother says on the phone late one afternoon. "This damned thing. I can't shower with it, and of course swimming is out of the question; I can't even sleep comfortably on it, it's such a big klutz." She's talking about her neck brace, which has become the focus and the curse of her life, sleeping and waking.

Since she has been living alone, I've tried to talk to my mother at least for a few minutes most days; usually she's in a hurry to get off the line and back to her life's work of making lists that will help her cope with chaos and confusion. "Yumm yumm, let's see," she'll say reflexively while looking over the index card of notes for things-to-say pinned to her refrigerator, before launching a thirty second synopsis of the class she's taking, the dinner with a friend she's had, the groceries available at Von's or Trader Joe's; and then she's ready to hang up, to release me back to the "important" activities of my day. "So go grade your papers," she'll say, "and don't forget to give everyone a big hug. Hugs are important."

"They are," I agree, stalling for time so I can find out more than the price of grapes in Southern California; "and of course I'll pass out your loving squeezes," I tell her. "But if you *really* loved me you wouldn't send me back to work." Usually I can cajole her into a few minutes more of chat about the lives of her friends that I have known or known about for decades but rarely see, about dinners she has shared with them, movies they have seen, concerts they have listened to together. Reassured that her days have more than half a minute's worth of value, I share with her the small stories of my own daily routines, of my wife's burdensome work responsibilities, of the melodramas and triumphs of her young-adult grandchildren as they make their ways into the world. And then we release each other with the promised hugs and expressions of love and affection.

But the accident has changed all that, and now conversations tend toward a tense dance of concern and complaint, with anxiety as much withheld as expressed. Neither of us will admit to a worry which, once expressed, would be difficult to defuse. We both fear an injury of sufficient seriousness to mark in some way the beginning of the end of the independence that has graced my mother's life into her mid-eighties. And we both fear the onset of a debilitating depression that is part of diminishment.

It was late afternoon on a soft and warm early autumn day when my sister called to tell me that my mother had been in an auto accident, but should be home from the hospital after an overnight of observations. The diagnosis we get the next day is fractured vertebrae, pronounced by a puffed neurosurgeon who is too busy to divulge much more information. It could be worse. My mother will have to wear a large collar-like brace, and stay out of the bath for a week, the pool for two months. She'll have to stay off her feet for a few weeks, and out of the driver's seat of any car until further notice. She frets that she can't remember much about the event, but she thanks God — with whom she hasn't had much official connection for nearly all the eight and a half decades of her life — over and over and over, grateful that the man driving the other car wasn't hurt.

Still bruised and shaken, her car hauled away for scrap metal, my mother is determined nonetheless to be fully functional on her own. Anxious not to burden anyone with her need for rides to doctors and shops, she has declared herself fit, a determination that's wonderful for its energy, a problem for its impracticality. Since the car accident, she says, she has been, not exactly dizzy, but tipsy, slightly off balance and fearful of falling when she stands up too suddenly, or turns too quickly. But she can manage, she says: "I'll take the bus. I'll walk slowly. I'll use my brother's cane."

This is the first I've heard of a family cane. Where, I wonder, was it hidden all the years of my growing up in a small apartment? It seems an odd keepsake for a woman who has been so determinedly neat and well organized that she has regularly thrown out or given away books, furniture, clothing, memorabilia, cookware, jewelry; who stores the daily newspaper in a trash recycling bag so that she won't forget to get rid of it next day; who has always been ceaselessly vigilant in her effort to make manageable the clutter of one small corner of the universe.

"I suppose I thought I might need it one day," she says when I ask her why she has carried this cane with her and so little else from coast to coast. "You never can tell when you're going to lose your balance." But the support, I discover, has less to do with keeping on your feet as you move through the daily routines of the present — however strong that necessity might be — than keeping an emotional balance by staying firmly in touch, always, with cherished presences from a past that's fading steadily with the passing years.

"It's a good cane," my mother says; "the wood's still strong and unblemished. And I feel like I need it to hold onto, especially when I get out of bed in the morning, when I think I'm going to fall flat before I can make it to the bathroom or the kitchen." I'm relieved that she has decided to use something for stability, and I tell her so, while she talks on about the cane, a dark wood with a high polish that's rubbed out a bit on the top curve of the handle; there hasn't been much wear and tear in the closet.

Abruptly her talk turns from the cane to her brother, about whom she has not said much before. "Did you ever meet Harry?" she asks. "Once," I remind her, "at my fifth birthday party." What I remember about him, besides his curly blond hair and his sweet smelling cherry blend pipe smoke, was a magic trick he performed again and again, seeming to bite off his thumb, then popping it back onto his hand. He took nickels from my ear, too, and made some marbles disappear under a cup. Neat stuff, I thought.

My mother says he died a few years after the war, from cancer brought on by war wounds. He was a hero, machine-gunned during the Battle of the Hedgerows. What I hear as she talks on, is that he was a hero to her long before the cataclysm of war, a golden boy worshipped then and now by his little sister.

Oh, A Beautiful Boy

"Oh, he *was* beautiful," my mother says to me one evening, looking over my shoulder at a trio of fading brown photographs of her brother that stand in a small semi-circle on her guest room dresser. In one, a clear-eyed child in shorts and a peaked cap looks like he's about to step into an *Our Gang* comedy of mischief and mayhem. An altogether more composed family portrait stands next to it. Here, his mother's hand rests on his shoulder, his sister's is around his waist. His father, pulled away slightly, looks on with patriarchal pride. In the third image, my uncle Harry, looking slender and weary, but crisply dressed in a starched military uniform, leans heavily on a dark cane, squinting into the light and holding hands with my mother, black-haired and girlish, with bright eyes and a determined smile. This one must have been taken at the VA hospital in the late 'forties, by which time my mother knew the clinical death sentence delivered to her brother.

"I remember going to the library on 42nd Street," my mother says, "and reading about melanoma when my brother wrote to tell me that he would be kept on at the hospital for awhile. Because he had been so shot up by the Nazis, he had been in a full body cast — not like they do it today, more like a barrel. He really couldn't move much; he could only roll around in the bed. We think that the recovery aggravated some birthmark that he had on his back. Anyway, I had to keep it to myself. I couldn't tell my mother or my father; they wouldn't have been able to stand it. I don't know how I did." My mother slides back, away from that moment, and tells me about how close she and her brother had been from earliest childhood.

"One summer," she says, "we finally got to visit my aunt in Philadelphia. We'd heard about the city of brotherly love for a long time, but we just hadn't had the money for all of us to leave Brooklyn. But then your grandfather gathered us all and announced that the children would go even if the adults couldn't. And so we were shipped off together to be with my aunt Fanny and her husband Max for a few weeks. Fanny had been in the Navy Waves, and Max had been a bantamweight boxer for the regiment. That's how they'd met and married, after one of Max's exhibition fights. Since the end of the war they'd returned to civilian life. Fanny was working at the Mint; Max was just hanging around, waiting, he said, for something to come along. And that summer, what came along was us.

"They had no children and were pleased to have us in for a few weeks. But we hadn't even been there for a day when the health department came to lock us in. Harry and I had been playing hide and seek out front, and it seems that one of the neighbors had noticed that Harry was limping. It was during the time of a Polio scare, and she hadn't wanted to do the obvious thing and ask these strange kids what might be the matter. So she called the health police who didn't ask us any questions, except how long Harry had been limping and where we were from. Harry had fallen and banged up his leg before we got on the train from New York. If they'd taken even a second to examine him, they'd have noticed the scrapes and bruises — the kind that kids always got. It was idiotic. But Max was down at the corner bar when they came, and Fanny was at work. And so they just ordered us upstairs and told us that we were quarantined; they left an official order on the kitchen table. I can't remember what we said later to Max and Fanny, or how they handled it. All I remember is that Harry and I were in the house together for days afterwards, and Harry read out loud to me and acted out stories, and we chased each other through the new rooms, hiding behind sofas and chairs while Harry pretended to be Robin Hood and I was a damsel in distress. We were never bored. Harry loved to read, and I loved to listen to him. Harry loved to be my hero and I loved to be rescued. It was the best holiday I could have wanted. Years later, Harry was still reading; I was still listening; we were still together wherever we were."

"Harry was like you," my mother says, "always with his nose in a book. Grandpa used to brag to everyone about how Harry was going to college, then graduate school. It was understood. There could be no other choice. He was so proud of Harry. And that's how it worked out. It's not that Harry had any ego about it. He always used to say that I should have been the one to go to college. That he'd have been fine without it; that he didn't need school to feel educated, just books."

"He was," my mother says, dreamy with the delight of memory, "brilliant."

It has always aggravated me to hear this. Because, after all, he *did* go to college, and my mother did not. She was pulled from school during the eighth grade because of the family's desperate need for money; they could only afford to cultivate one scholar, and that would be the exceptional male not the music-hungry female. Seven decades later she still talks about how much she enjoyed school before she was sent to work as a secretary for the Union. She remembers one special moment when she played piano in a junior high orchestra concert, when she was so frightened that she almost missed the performance, trying to find her way back from the girl's toilet in the dark hallways of the community center where the orchestra was waiting for her. "I told grandma and grandpa not to come see me," she says, still with some regret. "And they didn't." She seems surprised by it even now, thinking, I suppose, that she'd never have missed a performance of any kind by one of her children, no matter what they'd said in a flash of childish anxiety. "I played pretty well," she says proudly, "and I was asked to try out for some city-wide ensembles. But I never finished out the year." My mother alone of all her friends didn't go right on to high school and the possibility of Hunter College. Years later, when she was struggling to go back to night high school and my grandfather saw how much she wanted her education, he explained that he'd never have dragged her out of school at the age of twelve if he'd understood. "Grandpa taught himself to read *The New York Times* from cover to cover," she says; "he valued learning, and he loved me. But Harry was the true student. He was incredible, reading philosophy all the time, and those wonderful Modern Library editions of novels and poems. But he wasn't proud about it. He'd pass the books on to me after he'd read them. 'I'll be your school,' he'd say, but I couldn't really understand them, and I was busy at work."

I don't know what I want from my dead intellectual uncle or my long-gone impoverished grandfather, or even my quiet and modest mother. After all, a family crisis is a family crisis, and Harry and Ann were both children when the roads they traveled were mapped. But there's something that grates about my uncle's oh-so-easy dismissal of his own privilege after the fact, and my grandfather's sincere, but unenlightened, anguish at having limited his daughter, and my mother's predictably generous appreciation and forgiveness of those she loves.

I'd like to put my hands over my ears like the hear-no-evil monkey, and talk, not listen, when my mother offers her deep pleasure in her brother's accomplishments and her splendid sympathy for her father's paralyzing poverty. I'd like to say, but won't, "Harry was right, you should have been the educated child. You would have been an honors student; you're the student among us, the most deserving." Perhaps what annoys me most, after all, is that I *am* really just like that other Harry, having been oblivious or indifferent to my mother's loss and her promise, busy with my own things, accepting without real thought what she accepted, until I heard it thrown up at me in her sweet appreciations.

Determined to Walk

More than fifteen years after being pulled from school, my mother returned. Still working eight to five at the Amalgamated Union offices, she accelerated through a night school program that offered four years in two. It must have been thrilling and wearing to be getting on with it at last. For years she ran, swallowing large cups of coffee that kept her up long enough to do the homework that her friends had done as children. Her task lists became habitual. The vocabulary flash cards she made, the geometry proofs and numerical fact sheets that trailed behind her everywhere she went, marked the new terrain through which she stepped purposefully. Now, some sixty years later, after a stint at Bronx Community College and a slew of classes taken at Leisure World's Clubhouse Four, she is still walking with determination through the thickets of book learning. But lately, she tells me, her true walk has become unsteady.

"When I get to a corner, my right foot just freezes," she says to me on the phone. "I'll step down with my left foot first and then my other leg just won't move. I feel tipsy, like I'm going to fall flat on my face; so I'm caught between the sidewalk and the roadway, straddling the curb until someone can come along and offer me an arm or a helping hand. Yesterday I was there in limbo for fifteen minutes until I was rescued by a man on a bicycle." The fear in her voice frightens me. This one can't be joked away or talked away.

"Is it a balance problem?" I want to know. Or perhaps emotional? Can it still be related to the car accident? Perhaps it's time to get to a medical specialist, not just her HMO gatekeeper. In the days that follow, I notice that my mother gains strength and clarity while I lose it, my nervous fretting determined, perhaps, by my distance in far away England. Staying up late to reach the orthopedic surgeon, I'm filled with questions. He's polite in a busy sort of way, but his message is firm. "Your mother will need an operation to relieve pressure on her spine, and she'll need it soon," he announces. "Otherwise there's a serious risk of paralysis. We'll go in through the neck. She'll have trouble speaking for a week or so, but she should be out of the hospital in less time than that."

"But is that smart or really necessary for an eighty-eight year old woman?" I ask, resistant. "What are the risks? What are the chances of success and failure? What's the logic of it?"

"I *know* your mother's age," he says. "The logic is that momma is still an active woman; let's keep it that way. I wouldn't call for it otherwise," he explains, speaking in a voice that's a cross between professional peremptory and presumptuous personal.

"And if it doesn't take?" I ask.

"Well, that's not likely," he says with impatience at being challenged even this vaguely. "I've done lots of these. There's a small chance that it won't work, that she might need to wear a halo, a head and neck stabilizer that's drilled into the skull. But it's worth the risk. I'm sure momma would agree." Perhaps she would, because she's trained not to question educated authority, just as I'm trained to be impatient of it. But, in fact, he hasn't mentioned it to her, and won't; and she hasn't asked, and won't.

"That would kill her," I tell my wife when I'm off the phone. "She can't stand any enclosed spaces — elevators, toilet stalls, rooms without windows. Hell, she can't even take a CAT scan without a tranquilizer. And this enclosure would be attached to her. Never mind the pain." But my mother is ready and pragmatic, and wants it over. And so, despite much misgiving, I accept the inevitable.

Within a week of the surgery, she is up and about. Always expecting the worst, I am astonished by the miraculous turn. Within two weeks she is tuned back into *ER* and *The West Wing*. Within a month she is claiming full victory; except that she is still unsteady on her feet — "easily tilted," she says. The surgeon urges patience, a commodity that's perhaps hard to come by when you're less than two years shy of ninety and waiting for results. But when he suggests a quality walker to keep her on her feet, it seems the answer sprung fully and obviously to life.

Cruiser Deluxe

The fact that wheeled walkers are as common in Leisure World as the use of early bird special coupons at the local Black Angus Steak House has never persuaded my mother. These clever machines, equipped with hanging baskets for small grocery items, and a drop down seat for moments of great fatigue, have always seemed to her like a billboard announcing the end of stand-alone independence — a sign of moving one giant step closer to loss of self. She frets that people can't help but notice the sad degeneration of a fragile old woman propped up by an aluminum scaffold. But this time the need is great, the sense of urgency sharp.

Harry's cane is good for indoor use at best; and, having lost her car in the accident and decided it was time to give up her driver's license, she can't even pretend that she won't be housebound if she doesn't find a way to get about.

The thing is called an *Evolution Wheeled Cruiser Deluxe*, and conjures an image of scads of oldsters tooling round the sunny streets of Leisure World looking for a piece of the action, or swooping with speed and daring like Harry Potter on his super broom in a crucial Quidditch game. It's evolution beyond Darwin's imagining, and my mother is, after all, relieved to have found a place in the process.

In Stride

Lately I've been obsessed with family photos. It might be a function of memory loss, I think to myself, or the large distances over which our family is spread — England, Finland, the American West, Southwest, Northeast, Southeast. Or, most obviously, it's a consequence of the birth of my first grandchild in far off Helsinki. As if to remind myself who we all are, I periodically lay out dozens of pictures on the heavy oak dining room table that seems stable enough to bear the weight of all those days and years of experience. My current favorite is a Christmas snap that shows my newly-minted granddaughter, aged thirteen months, on her first and perhaps only visit to her great-grandmother in America. She's wearing a pair of brown overalls that my wife made for her father more than twenty-five years ago. Confidently, she struts across the front of the picture plane, leading her parents who amble along behind, ready to grab her should she stumble. In her right hand, she holds a small white propeller plane, ready for take-off. Her left hand squeezes my Uncle Harry's cane hard against her side. Hook-end forward, it rides before her like a giant baton ready to be handed off to someone just outside the photo. At the center of the picture frame, but behind the little parade, her great-grandmother waits, gripping her silvery walker. She stands at rest, stock-still and rock-steady, laughing with pure delight.

VIII

TALES MY FATHER TOLD ME

Family History

A friend called last night, laughing about his sister's efforts to chart a family history that goes back nearly four centuries in America, and is traceable in a family names book for another four hundred years before that in Ireland and England. He says she's following in the footsteps of some great aunt she's never met, who spent years searching records down in the damp of old churches and in attics thick with cobwebs and dust balls, looking for ancient letters in a failed attempt to wedge her way into membership in the Daughters of the American Revolution. He tells me that the record of the family tree, full branched but apparently inadequately rooted, is kept now in a ledger-sized book, bound in a grand red leatherette and distributed to immediate heirs and inheritors. While he talks on about his sister's serious hobby, I ponder my own family's thin record keeping. Sometimes I think there'd be no family history at all if it weren't for my father, who didn't have much history to tell, but who took immense delight in recounting it, real or fabricated. His voice became our oral record book, a thing constantly made and remade, just the sort of factual shenanigans that proper revolutionary daughters of the

Mayflower crossing loathed. Much of what I know is his knowing of people and places, newly alive with each retelling.

Doctor Doctor

My father, just turned eighty-six, is a quiet man, content with his own company and counsel, and capable of sitting for hours reading or listening to others less comfortable with silence chatter on around him. But once started, he loves to tell stories, and family gatherings have always been filled with the ritual of his tales told over and over to children and grandchildren for whom the predictable repetitions provide a steadying sense of stability.

Forever organized, and wanting to do his "job" faithfully and well, he has come east with a list of stories to share, complete with brief markings that I can't make out, annotations made in his tight, tidy handwriting. He is responding to my request that he put on record some of his favorites — for his family, for "posterity."

He wants to get it right, and seems not to trust his memory now. It's the way he has been, increasingly, for years — meticulously, almost disruptively, careful, responsible to the task at hand, like a thorough student with an assignment. When we talk on the phone on Sunday mornings, I'd swear

I can hear the index cards shuffling, each announcing a bit of information, an activity, some news. When I visit California, I get notes with directions for every trip I might need to make from the sanctuary of the retirement community out into the world of freeways and malls. And when I sit across the coffee table on this hot and muggy June morning, with a tape recorder whirring between us, I can feel the initial orchestrations as I tease him into voice.

"So before we get too far into this, Pop," I say, "maybe you can tell me who we are. I don't want metaphysical meanings, or psychobabble, just the facts, as Joe Friday used to say, just the facts."

I explain that I just received my annual flier today from a lady in Ohio who does family name books, "and for the modest sum of fifty bucks she says she can provide me with the Book of Martens — and I'm in it. You must be in it too, yes? Seems we have a grand and deep history going back centuries." I suppose *all* families go back centuries, but I know perfectly well that this one doesn't do it with the name Marten. "So what happened, Pop? How did we get this furry animal's moniker? I sort of know; I sort of remember; but I'm damned if I can hold on to the details since the last time you went over this stony ground."

What I remember most from that night years before, is that my sister and I and our spouses and some of our nearly grown children started with a smile of amazement, then a giggle, then uncontrollable laughter, while we sat around after dinner as my father went through the history of family name changing. After it, nothing was what it had seemed, and I was beginning to get a whole new take on the meaning of "find yourself." Marshall McLuhan once wrote that "The name of a man is a numbing blow from which he never recovers." Maybe so, but in our family it's not from want of trying.

"You know, I was almost Doctor Doctor," my father tells me, as if he's about to launch himself into a manic version of a Marx Brothers routine. What, you're feeling poorly? Call your Doctor, Doctor Doctor.

"I *do* remember that, Pop, more or less. You used to be Abe Doctor, which is not a bad name if you ask me. But did you really change the family name just because you thought you might go to graduate school and you didn't want to have an awkward name on the office door? Seems pretty drastic to play with basic identities that way. And besides, it's a long way from there to Marten with an "e," eh?" I say teasing. "Was it one of those Ellis Island immigration things?"

"Well, yes and no," my father explains, continuing to wrap me in a delicious ambiguity. "Of course our name wasn't really Doctor anyway. In fact, I don't even really know anymore what it was," he says, launching into the strange but commonplace tale once more. "Grandpa never talked about it; and I didn't think to ask. Names just didn't seem real or permanent. In my neighborhood, nobody's name went back more than a few years. Grandpa's brother was named Finklestein. I had cousins named Stein. Sometimes my uncles, aunts, cousins were called one thing, sometimes another. It seemed ok, but I suppose it wouldn't make much of a family tree book. Broken branches and bent limbs from the start. You remember when Grandpa came to New York he spoke only Yiddish and Russian. Of course the guy from immigration spoke English. I don't know that I could even spell it, but Grandpa once said that his given name was something like Dachtiar. I suppose that the officer who brought him into the country heard it as Doctor, and we all became instant MD's."

"Right, Pop, but Marten? You know: Gimme a 'D': 'M'; Gimme an 'ach': 'ar'; Gimme a 'tiar': 'ten.' Pretty confusing for cheerleaders, no?"

"Well," he continues," Grandpa had always said that he never liked his name, that it wasn't his. And his brother had come out of Ellis with a different name anyway, so there wasn't any given American name to protect. And neither Grandpa or his brother wanted to unite the family names — those guys disliked each other from way back. So when I graduated from college and I thought I was heading off to Columbia for a Ph.D., Grandpa said it was the right time for us to become something different, something that wasn't even pretending to be close to the Russian family name, and something that wouldn't sound silly with all the doctors we were sure to have in the family before long. We all met with my cousin who was a lawyer, and decided on Grandpa's father's name, which was Martin. But Martin the usual way with an "i" seemed too English for us, and Grandpa wouldn't have it, so he changed the spelling to an "e." We had no idea that there was an animal; there were no furry martens on the lower east side. And we had no idea that if it wasn't English it would be something else, like Dutch, or Danish, sometimes with two "a's," sometimes with an "s" at the end. While we were at it, throwing out the identities of our first decades in the new world and starting over like real Americans, my brother Carl decided to change his name from Sam; I think he wanted something Germanic so he could get a job with the telephone company. And while the lawyer had all the papers out, I discovered that my real name was Avrom not Abraham, and that I had a middle name I'd never used, never heard: Abba."

Though I know the basic outlines of the story, I have the same sense of vertigo as I listen to it again, that I had before when it was all a revelation — as if things I'd known, people I'd known, weren't themselves any more, and never could be any more. Who the hell was my uncle Sam, a phantom figure that looked like young Carl? My father Avrom Abba, echoes of some distant tongue? My grandfather Dachtiar Doctor calling a family pow-wow to perform the revolutionary act of naming himself? How close was I to being Finkelstein?

How would I have liked being Doctor Doctor to my students? Thoreau, who had a word for everything, once wrote that "A name pronounced is the recognition of the individual to whom it belongs. He who can pronounce my name aright, he can call me, and is entitled to my love and service." But if I go to the front door of family memory now, and call Avrom, Abba, Sam, Dachtiar, Doctor, who will recognize the syllables and answer back?

The Jailbird Sequence

"For a solid citizen, Pop, you seem to have had a pretty checkered past," I say after lunch. "How about this afternoon we do a jailbird run?"

Looking down at his notes, he begins as if he's had a sudden revelation: "Have I told you about the time I was shaken down by the cops?" he asks.

"Of course you have. But I'd like to hear it again. There's a horse thief hanging on every family tree; and I guess for ours you're it, eh?" I smile as he gathers momentum and offers a portrait of an unenthusiastic rebel swept helplessly along in a world of unsettling arbitrary injustices.

The images come quickly: my father at twelve having come to the schoolyard to play basketball, suddenly running from he doesn't know what, as barrel-chested plainclothes detectives roust a local craps game and sweep up everyone in sight, clobbering them as they crawl, single-file, through a hole in the fence and back out to the street. I can picture it like an old *Our Gang* comedy: "chickee, the cops." But though my father nods toward bemusement, he clearly isn't laughing hard at the humiliation, even more than seven decades later. At fourteen, history repeats: the high school freshman wanders past a pool hall and into trouble as he's caught, while gawking at the melodrama, in a police shakedown of neighborhood gamblers. Frightened, but having no cash to offer up to the "bulls," gods of law and order, he's spread-eagled — hands high against the wall, frisked, and sent on his way with a New Yorker's increasingly clear recognition of the need to mind your own business, and a steady but respectful dislike of authority.

It's not just kid stuff, my father wants me to know. "When your mother came out of the hospital after her first surgery," he says, "I took her over to Van Cortlandt Park, just to relax on the grass. It took about two minutes to drive over; she was sad and tired and weak. I helped her out onto the lawn and then went back for a chair. We weren't even out of sight of the car. But before I could blink, a cop was writing up a ticket for the car which he said wasn't supposed to be parked there. What got me was that he said I'd been there for hours. It was just as long as it took me to bring mother a chair, no more than a minute at most. I began to argue with him, and mother came over, and finally he said he'd let us off this time, but don't do it again. Do *what* again, try to get mother a few minutes ease in the park? Those guys are never satisfied, always trying to get everything they can."

The bitter edge passes as he picks up again on the absurdity of finding himself — so solid a citizen — again and again wrapped in the tight embrace of the long arm of the law. No memorable moment tickles his fancy more than his being caught by the subway police with a book.

"You know," he tells me, "I was just curious, just wondering what was going on. That's all, I mean it." It seems he'd just come down onto the station platform near Penn Station, and saw several guys in identical black rain coats going through peoples' pockets. "I suppose I should have kept moving, but I was wondering what sort of swindle was in progress. One of the raincoat guys noticed me, flashed me his badge, put his hand on my side and felt a book I'd been carrying. He wanted to know what it was, and when I told him it's a book, he said, 'and just what the hell are you doing with that?' I tell you, I was astonished. 'Reading it, I'm reading it,' I explained. But he still seemed angry and suspicious. He wanted to see some identification and I wanted to reach for some, but he wouldn't let me reach into my pocket, even to take out the book. He kept asking and he kept threatening every time I made a move to give him what he wanted. It went like that for a long time, and finally he just said, OK, be on your way. He was toying with me, I think. Maybe his lesson was that old one about book learning: a little knowledge can be a dangerous thing, eh?"

One Strap Down

A feel of frustration and puzzlement — a sort of willfully exaggerated "what am I doing here?" perplexity — fills these tales, vocal warm ups to my father's favorite account of a brush with the law: his lurid tale of "Indecent Exposure."

He says "it all started with some girls who rented a bungalow in Peekskill." They had invited him and few friends up for a weekend, but being girl shy he spent most of his time off by himself, hiking the nearby hills, or swimming in a lake a mile or so from the cottage. It was the swimming that did it, he says. He could hear the whistle and yelling before he saw the squat beefy guy waving at him from the shore, gesturing cartoon-like toward a car parked just off the sand. "I couldn't make out a word he was saying," he tells me, "but he had to mean me, because I was the only one anywhere around, even though I was in the middle of the lake."

"When I finally got out," he continues, "with water puddling at my feet, I could see he was a cop. All he said was 'get into the rumble seat.' No explanation, not even a gesture toward civility. But there was a little boy there in the rumble seat, too — about ten years old — who didn't know what was going on either. All the cop said was 'you'll find out, you'll find out,' like I was also ten years old and was being told to wait till my father came home."

In the town six miles away, my father explains, there was a music store — smack in the middle of the one block long main street. The shopkeeper, it turns out, was the town judge, and my father was, as he puts it, "flabbergasted" to find that he was being charged with indecent exposure. "I just could-n't understand," he tells me, as indignant now as he had been more than six decades ago. It seems he had been caught in the water with one strap down, and one strap down was enough. He'd been trying to relieve the rub on a sunburned shoulder, and thinking that the middle of a lake was a pretty secure place to do what you pleased, he'd lowered that damned strap. Besides, he wanted to know, "who says you can't swim with a strap off?" In East Hampton, the men were swimming without tops at all. "And where were the rules posted?" he wanted to know. They were up outside the store, six miles from the water's edge. Literally trembling with remembered exasperation, he says into the tape recorder: "if you're going to have a rule about swimming why not post it where the swimmers can see it? And I was in the middle of the lake, for God's sake. I was alone. If I was in a bathtub in my own house, would that be indecent exposure?"

"Just imagine what a charge of indecency would

have done to me" — he asks me to think it through, then goes on with the tale. "Well, you seem like an intelligent guy," the judge had said, his bald head sweating and his Americana bow tie bobbing. "I tell you what — the fine is usually $35, but just this time I'll make it $10. And $10 for the boy, too."

"I didn't want to pay a plug nickel,' my father tells me, "not one damned cent." The alternative was simply a weekend in jail, and intelligent guy that he was, my father agreed to the fine. What happened next has my father laughing, but in the quiet of the morning I can almost hear his teeth grinding as he tells it: "So the fat lawman drives us off to get our cash, stopping for the kid first. Well of course the kid's no dummy, and he disappears when he gets out to find money to pay for his crime. That leaves me, and the cop's not about to let me out of his sight. He walks me into the cottage while I go for my money, listens to piles of protest from the girls, pockets the cash, and takes off with the rumble seat empty, ready to be filled with another city sucker."

The amazement still rings in his voice. I don't think it's just a measure of his surprise and anger at being had by rubes, an urban pride popped by the sharp edge of a rural scam — though that certainly still rubs him wrong. Or that it's just one more cynical tale of the way the system inevitably screws you, though his stories are filled with object lessons like that. I think the event is so strongly marked for this man whose young adulthood was defined by the death of his wife in her early thirties — an event he hardly ever talks about, that left him financially and emotionally flattened by her two years of slow dying and by the need to raise two infants by himself for a time — because it says, in a way he *can* talk about, that you're never safe, even minding your own business, even in the middle of a lake, even when you play by the rules as you know them.

Guns and Guns and Guns and Guns

When I was in the sixth grade, there was a TV western I liked that began with a camera shot of an empty-looking frontier landscape, and a song celebrating an American need and the American way. Sometimes bits of the tune still pop into my head. "A lawman came with the sun," is what I remember: "there was a job to be done, and so they sent for the badge and the gun — of the LAWMAN." Though I can still see Palladin clearly from "Have Gun, Will Travel," and of course, Matt Dillon and Wyatt Earp, I have no picture for this man who goes with the badge and the gun. But his facelessness suits. Part of the six-gun myth, there to serve and protect, he's planted in my mind as a vague figure foregrounded against piercing sunlight, jostling for psychological elbow room alongside my father's pictures of the corrupt cops much closer to home than the wild west.

But violent epic redeemers and small scale abusers of the public trust aren't the only players in the gun game. As if to find a space between TV's glorifications and his own annoyed debunkings — to remind his children that, for an average guy, guns and contacts with men who play with guns are best left alone — my father's tales turned early and often to self-deprecating, anti-macho portraits of his own waltz with weapons.

"I'd never really touched a gun," he says. "It was not a Bronx thing to do."

Like keeping a dog in the city, I suppose, or a car. I don't remind him of the gangsters he has told me about who grew up in his neighborhood — guys with names like "Dutch" and "Legs," who wound up in the Tombs or dead. And I don't mention the unsettling images from my own teenage nights on Mosholu Parkway — shadowy pushers like Herbie who sold to fourteen-year-olds until he was way past thirty, and who was shot and killed on the little strip of grass in front of Junior High School 80, found during lunch break one autumn morning; or the knife-flashing, gun-toting, bicep-popping members of the Bronx's biggest and baddest gang — the comically named but very unfunny Fordham Baldies who swooped in from the east to thrill and terrify us. Nor do I remind my father of the obvious facts about "Bronx things" now in the 'nineties; even in the secure bastion of his retirement community in Orange County, the newspapers do that every day.

"ROTC was a required class at City College, but even that was gunless," he says, "until the annual target walk." He warms to the subject, his body straightening with a kind of self-mocking military air.

"We wore uniforms," he says, "and had to say cadet so-and-so, company so-and-so, asks permission to speak, and we walked stiff and were supposed to look serious and dangerous. But guns? Nope. Except on the day we were marched off to the target — one time only during the year. One day a year, and one gun."

There were only about twenty-five cadets left, he explains, by the time they'd shuffle-marched across campus to the gym where the firing range was set up; if you weren't within clear sight of the sergeant you just dropped away somewhere near 139th street. It was a company of the misplaced unlucky by the time the platoon leader lined them up and pulled out the single heavy pistol reserved for their use. Because my father was standing near him, so the story goes, he was handed the gun first, was pointed toward the target, was told to go ahead and shoot.

"That was it for instruction," my father says. "So what's the big deal? I pointed and popped, and hit the ceiling dead center." He hadn't realized that the thing had such a kick, but being a well-coordinated and smart lad, he knew that his second shot would be better. But there was no second shot — one day a year, one gun, one bullet. "Colin Powell came out of that program," my father says; "he must have been a good intuitive shooter."

My father wore his misfiring like a badge of pride; and a year later "they sent for the man with the badge and the gun." Like many trying to get by during the years of the Great Depression, my father had taken a job with the central post office in midtown Manhattan. Faced with thousands of mail bags, absurdly ordered to "shake out them coupla sacks," my father found himself one evening pleased to be yanked off the loading floor and into security duty. It seemed a more civilized way to work the late shift, and might even allow time for some reading before the next day's classes. "Take this gun," his shift supervisor said, "and follow me."

"Follow me" is one of my father's favorite story lines. It seems to catch the essential absurdity of things that runs through all his narratives. You haven't a clue? Follow me. You don't know where? Follow me. You don't know how? Follow me. Whenever I hear "follow me" I know that a hopeless, hapless, event will surely follow along with me. "This needs protection," the shift foreman had said, pointing to a large armored mail truck heading out to the boroughs.

"I didn't get it," my father tells me, chuckling, "but, hey, it seemed better than heaving sacks. Still, I can tell you I was not about to confront any bad guys, and I was not about to shoot my foot off, either. I'd fired a gun once; I guess that made me about as expert as anybody around the place that night. But an empty gun is a wholesome gun, I say, and so I put the box of bullets he gave me into my pocket, and I put the gun through my belt in the back of my pants. It was uncomfortable, but at least I wasn't about to fire the thing off by mistake, even if I sat down hard. That's a sure way to strip your gears."

"I *told* him I wouldn't load the gun," my father remembers with a rolling of his eyes. "All he answered was: 'look pal, I just hand it out; what you do with it is your business.' That's how I became the mail truck sheriff. We never saw any gangsters; we never saw anybody. I suppose all the valuable mail was ripped off before it even got to the trucks. I'm pretty sure that all we were carrying were letters from Cohen to Stein, or O'Leary to Murphy — news of the neighborhood, important but not worth a shooting. I felt ridiculous carrying bullets in my pocket and a gun at my hip, but I'm glad I couldn't have shot anyone even if I'd had to."

"Have bullets in pocket," reads the card of the postman — a long, long way from Palladin.

And Gladly Did He Teach

But that's not to say that New York wasn't a threatening place. When my father at last traded-in his midnight holster for chalk and grade books, he only just began to comprehend the many ways the city of immigrant dreams and hard awakenings could intimidate and frighten its citizens, even when they were not facing trouble that might have sprung from the pages of *True Detective* or the city's favorite tabloid, *The Mirror*.

My father, a frustrated scholar of Romance languages, must have been surprised one morning to discover himself facing hordes of indifferent teenagers with a whistle in his hand, dressed in the peculiar baggy disguise of a gym teacher. I don't mean that he wasn't expecting it, but that it still must have shocked him. Faced with the impossibility of finding work as a French teacher in a city that spoke dozens of dialects of English but had little interest in supporting the speech of foreigners, and effete European foreigners at that, my father — despite his years of undergraduate and graduate learning — had done what any of us would have done: he made a virtue of necessity. An exceptional athlete, he retooled even before he'd had a chance to reach into his bag of academic tricks; and with a year of intensive classes in tests and measures, baseball, and the physiology of the hop, step, and jump, he sprinted his way into a job coaching track and teaching physical education at several schools in Brooklyn and the Bronx.

Judging from my own encounters with gym teachers whom I remember with mixed degrees of affection as "Black Mike," "Coach Slab," and just plain "D-uh," I realize that my father must have felt himself cosmically transplanted from the sweet troubadour songs of Bertrand de Born to the shrill tune of "listen up you guys." In some ways his life became a kind of willful forgetting of his early language and literary interests, though he must have been the most linguistically driven coach in the history of Evander Childs High School track: "Coach Verbs" would be my guess. And as the most literate teacher of athletes in the school system, he was soon off to administrative jobs and to a college post in physiology. But the years of working with teams of teens defined him in ways that decades of curriculum development in health education couldn't match.

I Paid Two Fares

Playground ball is what they call it — after-school sports on cement basketball courts, watched over by a moonlighting teacher who's exhausted but needs every job he can get to supplement a salary that barely brings home the bacon. My father did it for years in Harlem, hopping the El right after his day in the northeast Bronx, hauling his whistle, his rule books, and his love of games as baggage into alien territory.

Over the years, the huge greetings that had gone up within a week of his first arriving — orange painted on the handball wall: "Marten Is a Pinhead," "Marten Don't No Diddly" — had faded into a soft, almost shadowy dirty brown scrawl. But he could still make it out, and found it oddly comforting in its familiarity as he unlocked the gated fence to the schoolyard every afternoon. He worked with any of the kids who wanted some attention, showing them how to set a pick, or bank a hook off the boards. But for the most part his work was keeping the pushers out of the yard.

One day, though, was different, memorable. Something between a coach and a hall monitor, he'd selected a team of "all stars" to play in a city tournament up near Fordham Road. What he remembers, he says, is that his kids won easily, but they were miserable. Going out of the neighborhoods, playing whites in a white school, was scary. There were no incidents that he remembers, no fights even. But my father's recognition that the city was a patchwork of isolating fortresses, even in the good old days before the race wars heated up, stays with him.

As he tells it, the day of the tournament the "all stars" and "coach don't no diddly" headed off to an uptown trolley for the long ride to the front. His players were popping with machismo, and had picked up war names in readiness for the fight: Bullet, Bombs, Tank, Slash, Speed. There was lots of trash talk, and when my father got his battalion of children to the trolley, he gave each road warrior a nickel for fare, to drop into the box before moving on back. Chattering and pushing, they piled on, leaving my father and the conductor to bring up the rear. Both were surprised, though perhaps they shouldn't have been, to find only one nickel in the box when they climbed up the step.

"So who's paying?" my father was asked, and as he told his story I had visions of one of the great fantasy moments of my childhood, when I'd imagined going to Yankee Stadium and pointing to the friend behind me, then he would point, then his friend, as we filed in, all saying "he's got the tickets," until we were all home free and spreading out through the grandstands. Of course it never worked like that for me, hard as I imagined it. But there they were, my father and the conductor, shooing the mighty all stars out of the trolley, lining them up again, and asking them which one of them had paid. All of them had paid, was the word. But all of them had to pay again before they could climb back on board.

"I paid two fares" was the cry all the long way to the Bronx and all the victorious way back.

"Two, count 'em, one — two. *Two* fares!"

"How many, Speed?"

"Two, man, I paid *Two Fares*."

"Bombs? Slash? Bullet?"

"Two, I say, T-W-O. I ask you: Is that *FAIR*?"

When they finally hopped off the trolley, comfortable again at home and determined to screw the system that was screwing them, the winners copped fruits and finger food from the street vendors as they crowded past on their way back to the playground. Apparently my father didn't subscribe to the notion of "to the victors go the spoils," though, and his tour of homes — talking to parents, grandparents, guardians about the grocers' complaints — earned him a new entry on the handball wall of fame: "COACH TWO FARES IS A BASTARD," a bright red paint job brushing its way into family history.

A Good Crease

Like most teachers I've known, my father generally dressed the part. Though both of his wives saw to it that he was lovingly and properly outfitted for a day in front of teens and civil servant colleagues, he managed almost instantly to transform suits from Brooks Brothers into rumpled cloth. He didn't cultivate the lived-in look, it just stuck to him. My father tells me that my biological mother, Elizabeth, an intense, fiercely articulate woman, understood that he had no sense of style — "it was like food," he says, "whatever was put in front of me was fine, and I was color blind on top of it." She would brook no debate about which tie, hat, socks, shoes, went with which jacket. My stepmother, Ann, made getting my father out the door in sartorial splendor one of the marks of her marriage. But by day's end, he'd come back to the family fold looking as if he'd been asleep in his clothes in the park. In the heartland of Madison Avenue chic, my dad remained something of a rehab project, but comfortable with himself, and glad to be of use to those in need of a project. Too, being a shy man, he seemed genuinely pleased that his lack of flash protected him, kept him out of public notice. But sometimes you just get tangled in your safety net, especially in New York where you may never know you're walking a wire until it's too late to back off.

"Back in the 'thirties, New York had a World's Fair," my father says, as if it's news, by way of introducing one of his many "things aren't always what they seem" stories.

"I had gone with your mother out to Flushing Meadows to spend the day finding out what was new in the world. There were lectures, shows, demonstrations, long lines, large crowds. Elizabeth and I stopped where a fellow was demonstrating some kind of portable pressing gadget, a sort of small clamp he'd run up and down your trousers to make a crease. I was just one of a huge number of people watching, but the guy who was running it called me forward. Before I had any idea of what he was up to, he put this gadget on my leg."

"But Pop," I say, "how could you not know what he was up to? What did you think he was doing?"

"Well, maybe I thought he was trying to give me one for nothing."

"Ah, Pop, how could you grow up in the city and think that?"

"Really, I suppose I just wasn't thinking at all; I didn't think of it as a street scam because this was a World's Fair after all — in all the papers, attended by hordes of people, a celebration of all that was new and exciting and good in the world, and I'd hardly ever even been outside of the city. Anyway, he ran it up and down the leg of my pants and made a real crease on one side."

"Just out of curiosity, Pop," I interrupt, "and in the name of scientific discovery, what kind of pants were you wearing? Cotton pants? Wool? Dress slacks? Some cutting edge synthetic fabric?"

"Well obviously I was wearing the kind of pants that needed a crease," my father says, straight-faced. "And he began to use me as a demonstration to this huge crowd. Normally I'm the sort of person who would like to stand in the back. I didn't like being the subject of all the curiosity. After he got through demonstrating on one side, he began to explore the possibility of selling some of these things. World's Fair, phooey. He was just a pitch-man, a huckster, and I was the poor sod selected to bring joy and enlightenment to his flock. I had to stand there for more than a half hour with one crease in my pants, while he talked to the group, trying to enlist their financial support. Eventually he exhausted his pitch and everybody left. And I looked down and there was one pants leg crisp and showy, and one baggy and sagging. So I said what about the other leg, and he said, 'don't worry, we'll take care of it.' Then I realized, with horror, what he was up to. He began to call people over. He'd taken about forty-five minutes to do the one side, and now would take another forty-five to finish the job. I was stuck there for more than an hour and a half. All the time I was thoroughly embarrassed because I was front and center. He ran up and down the other side, and eventually I had both sides creased. He wanted to sell the thing to me. All I could say was get me the hell out of here."

"What about mother," I ask, "she must have found the whole thing very amusing in an aggravated sort of way."

"She didn't say a word," my father remembers.

"That's funny, she could be so outspoken."

"We moved on to this place where they were selling cooking utensils. You remember the TV adds for knives that dice and slice without ever getting dull? Well this was something like that. And the salesman was trying to beckon the crowd forward. But I was not about to move. I figured I don't know what he's starting to show exactly, but he wasn't going to stick me again. My stylishly crisp trousers and I stayed out of sight, out of harm's way. I'd had my fifteen minutes of fame."

Hats and Sewers

It's clear to me as I listen to him, that my father's persona is that of a perplexed but unsurprised and right thinking man holding on for dear life while capricious winds whip past him. He cherishes every gust. Still, his grip is firm — especially on his hat.

What you have to know about my father is that he has been about as bald as a man can be since he was nineteen. An early brown and white photo shows him with his brother at Rockaway Beach, deeply tanned, tightly muscled, smiling, and reflecting a bright glare off what he has gingerly called his bald spot. No other pictures are as naked. By the time he was a young father, he had a brown Stetson firmly in place, not to be easily dislodged for anyone or by any weather. But sometimes men and nature just play tricks.

One of the delights of my own life has been to sneak that hat off and kiss and rub his head for luck and love. It got easier as my father got older and shorter, shrinking into himself. His head was a radiant, scrumptious target below my eye level as I stepped beside him, or when we hugged in greeting. Sometimes, though, others got to the hat first.

"So, pop," I say, tilting the peak of his new California-blue senior citizen's golf cap slightly askew, "have you ever had a hat tragedy? Gone without?"

"Only twice," he tells me. "When you're as light on the top as I am, you'll appreciate the importance of cover. I even sleep with a cap. A man needs protection from the elements." But it just doesn't always work out.

He doesn't begin like Bulwer-Lytton or Snoopy with "it was a dark and stormy night," but he conjures the same feel of nature gone amuck and charged with impending disaster. "I can't remember a wetter day," he says. "My pants were sticking to my legs like wet leaves. The rain was straight at you, horizontal. It was like that all the way up Jerome from Mosholu Parkway. Nobody was out, and I was thinking that I wouldn't be either in a few more minutes. The stores were empty all the way up the block. Everyone was hustling along, head down to keep the rain out of their eyes, to avoid puddles and dog feces. I just wanted to be done with it. You know, I was only a hundred feet from the house, and holding on with one hand to my briefcase and the soggy lumps of the *Times* and *Telegram* I'd been reading on the subway. And I was trying to hold my coat together at both the top and bottom too." While he talks, I see Dickens's "implacable November weather," Melville's "damp, drizzly November in [the] soul," even though it's warm and still all through the room we're sitting in now.

"You remember the hill on 212th?" he asks. "Where the egg man lived, and walked his dogs that crapped up the neighborhood? Well, I was just at the top of it when my hat was whipped off my head even though I made a grab for it. It rolled over those damned poodle turds and straight for the corner where the big sewer was, and right down into it. It was brand new; it had a nice new tight fitting plastic rain cover on it; it was set for anything." He's laughing now, deep down chuckles. "I just stood there, looking; I could see it, like a drowned rat, but I couldn't believe it."

"It was the hat that your mom got me right after those kids lifted my other one," and he's off on the story behind the story. "You know we didn't get a lot of new stuff in those days, but mom was determined that I would go to work looking smart. She knew exactly what she wanted for me when we went down to Wallach's, and I knew that what she wanted, I wanted. I hadn't been wearing that hat for two weeks when it was lifted right off my head at the 161st Street IRT station by some high school kids who'd been cutting up since they got on at 125th. They all had book bags, and they were swinging them against each other in wide arcs that cleared a fairly good-sized space on the train. I wasn't paying much attention; I'd gotten on down near Canal Street, so I had a good seat and I was reading. But I think most people were relieved to see the back of them when they all piled out by Yankee Stadium. It worked the other way for me."

"The windows were wide open because the train stank, and was blowing foul air from the heating vents under the seats. When the doors closed behind them, the kids just reached in from the platform, grabbed my hat and ran down the stairs."

"You mean they left you naked, Pop?" I say. "The villains."

"I pulled the switch to stop the train," he continues, unflappable: "And the conductor came running back. But since the emergency was to *my* head, and since the kids must have been long gone by that time, and since I was holding up the wheels of New York's fine public transportation, he just let me know that I could file some paper work about it if I wanted to — if I wanted, unaccountably, to waste more of my presumably valuable time, that is. Two weeks later I was looking down into the sewer, watching my next new hat float like a proud boat on dark waters."

"And what then?... a *new* new hat?," I joke. "That's more extravagant than the *Cat in the Hat*, Pop. Maybe you needed a helmet, not a fedora. Or maybe you just needed to face the world uncrowned, eh?"

"Well, it *is* a war out there," he says with a smile, "and there are always Emperors running around with their new clothes on, but you wouldn't want to send your old dad out into the world without protection, would you?"

To the End of the Line

We lived at the end of the line. Take the "D" train to 206th, or the IRT to Woodlawn. Walk up streets with oddly exotic sounding names — Bainbridge, Gun Hill, Rocheambeau, Kossuth, or past the green of the huge old cemetery sprawling at the edge of the drab apartments like a private park. "If you are not happy with your present location, you may request a transfer," one Woodlawn Cemetery sign read, but as far as I could tell, inside the gates and outside, people tended to stay put. The subway carried us out — to school, or work, or play — but it always brought us back through the same dank tunnels to the familiar steadiness of home territory. The subway looms large in family legend and lore — maybe because we all spent so much time on it, and things happen where you spend your time. Maybe because it was our link with the larger world, and that world was a place of our imaginings. Maybe because it was a pressure release valve that enabled us to remain pleased with our confined neighborhoods while feeling that we could move along at any time and be biting into somebody else's piece of the city pie. Maybe because it was unpredictable. Like my father with his hat suddenly disappearing down the platform stairs, the subway exposed and revealed us.

Though it took me one snowy Christmas to Carnegie Hall to see the Weavers in concert, and often to the Five Spot Café for Thelonious Monk and friends — though it rode me down to the West Eighties where I could get a glimpse of the antique laden, plush apartments of much richer high school friends, and down to my cousin's place on Houston Street where there was always Jim Beam waiting and I could pretend with his NYU pals that I was older, smarter, more experienced than I could imagine — this underground railroad came to seem like a twisted fairyland: risky, troubling, magical.

My worst subway year by far was my first year of high school. Because my father had gone to Stuyvesant, a special science school in the depths of lower Manhattan — because I'd grown up with paternal choruses of "Stuyvesant Will Shine Tonight" sung with surprising enthusiasm — I took the entrance test and found myself riding the iron rail at 6:15 to be on 14th Street before 8:00. From mid-autumn to late winter it was dark when I sleep-walked onto the train at Woodlawn Station, and dark when I came home at 6:00 after fencing practice. The sunny day seemed to be a thing that happened somewhere else while I was in school cooking some color-changing liquid in my Bunsen burner, like a hapless embodiment of one of MacBeth's witches about to break into chant: "Double, double toil and trouble; / Fire burn, and cauldron bubble."

The light I remember that year was artificial classroom light, and glaring underground station light. Sometimes there would be a flashing comet-tail that snapped and crackled around a skinny Asian selling glow-in-the-dark, battery-charged, sun-yellow Yo-Yo's during the fifteen minutes everyday when the train stopped with its lights out just in front of Grand Central Station. Or a red, white, and blue sparkle in the whirring flag waved by the tiny wind-up soldiers who walked in circles in the passageway to the street at Union Square: "hey you, Red (my hair? my politics?), ain't ya got no pride in our country? Bring one of dese home and show your mudder ya love America."

There was always pushing and grunting as the crowd, rushing to get away from home, then rushing to get home, packed itself tighter into the subway car; and there were some memorable fights, like the one between two girls on the platform at 149th — screeching, hair pulling, eye gouging, and finally knives, while everyone miraculously scattered to make room where it seemed a moment before that you couldn't slip a piece of paper between bodies. But for the most part, the thin light set off the uniform colorless world of fellow travelers breathing in shallow unison, shuffling together like some newly made huge monster worm that slides through the airless passageways of the dark tunnels.

In the spring of that year, when my chemistry lab partner suddenly made news headlines — "Honors Student Arrested For 3 AM Bombing of Telephone Booth in Grand Central Station" — I experienced an authentic "Aha! phenomenon." Eureka, as they say in the world of scientific discovery. It revealed what I had suspected all along — that while I had been trying without success to make the liquids in my test tube turn blue or pink or red, he had been doing something very, very different — and, oddly, it all made perfect sense to me: the act, the target, the perverse use of natural gifts — in a weird way, a gesture of survival and defiance from one of the underground men. By then I'd had enough of subterranean wanderings myself, and decided to transfer to the science high school in the Bronx, where I could walk to work, and venture onto the subway only when I chose a change. Stuyvesant still "shines tonight" in the world behind my father's eye, but not with enough wattage to light and brighten my memory through the tunnels that lead the way there.

The Best Thing

Nearly four decades later, though, the IRT redeems itself wholly in my father's improbable tale of love made possible by mechanical breakdown. It has been a long afternoon of tape recorded chat, and I suggest that enough's enough. I know he's enjoying the encore retellings of the stories of his lifetime, and he doesn't want to let me down; but he's clearly weary. And so I shut the tape recorder down and we head off for seltzer. But he insists that I click on for one more tale: "I want to tell you about the best thing that happened to me. When the train died at 161st."

Slowly, ceremonially, weighing his words in a way that even as a careful wordsmith he hasn't up to now, he explains to the waiting machine, to me leaning toward the mike, to my mother quietly listening on the sofa, "I wasn't looking for mom, but she was there on the platform when the conductor herded us all out of the train. She was living on 161st and she was just heading down the stairs. I was getting ready to wait on the platform in the November cold for a new train to get me the rest of the way home." I remember a bit of the story of how just before my birth mother, Elizabeth, died, she had "selected" mom for my father's next wife. I used to think it was improbable; it makes perfect sense to me now with the hindsight of decades. I applaud Elizabeth's courage, common sense, insight, looking into the heart of her own darkness. They had all been summer friends before mom's first husband died suddenly of heart failure. And when Elizabeth was herself hospitalized with a melanoma that had metastasized, and knew for a certainty that she'd be dead within a year, so the story goes, she took my dad in hand and let him know amidst all the other organizing that was to go on, that he'd have to find a new wife and mother, and that Ann Miller was the one and no other.

"No other" was the way it seemed it would be for awhile, as my father, devastated by loss and financially broken, all but lost himself in working long days at school, and long nights and weekends at seeing to the needs of his confused children. None of us have talked about it much, except to kid him about his hunt for a woman who'd have him with two kids in tow. But he speaks steadily now, looking right at my mother across the room. She joins in, forming a lovely, loving counterpoint.

"We only talked for a minute," she says, "but he called me at home before suppertime and we went out that night."

"That night? That night? Why you old swifty you," I kid my father. "I guess you knew what you wanted. But why did you wait so long, Pop? I have a feeling that if you hadn't met mom on the platform by accident that afternoon, we'd all still be waiting for a new woman of the house."

"I was so busy, I didn't know whether I was coming or going," he says. I wasn't thinking about women; I was thinking about you and your sister. But when I saw mom, I remembered. For you. For your sister. For me."

"I don't think Dad would have remarried," my mother says, "except for you and Beth."

"Well, lucky we put the squeeze on you, Pop."

My mom, family legend has it, won my sister with her Steinway, which traveled with her to our apartment in the Bronx. She won me with her spaghetti, which I consumed with enough steady relish to turn from worried looking reed to smiling butterball in less than a year. And she won my father by being, as he says, again and again into the rolling tape recorder of our family history — by being the best person in this whole cockeyed world; the best thing that ever happened to him; the best thing he could ever have imagined happening to him.

This Is My Box

When I was ten years old I fell in love with Gian Carlo Menotti's Christmas opera *Amahl and the Night Visitors*. We didn't celebrate Christmas as a religious holiday, rather as a kind of nationally sanctioned occasion for gift giving and family friendship. I had no interest in either opera or tales of the baby Jesus. But I'd heard the music on the radio and couldn't get it out of my head. And so I was pleased and excited to wake up on Christmas day to find on top of my mother's upright piano, where gifts were placed in the absence of a tree, my first adult record: lovely, lively music, rich with the delight of wise men and peasants singing and dancing, celebrating the miracle of birth and recovery from crippling illness. I relished it all, playing the disc over and over again, hour by hour.

Decades later, when I became a parent and was dealing with children who sometimes just wouldn't do what they were told, I often found myself surprised to be singing softly to myself the mantra of Amahl's mother's lament: "What shall I do with this boy? What shall I do? What shall I do?" But the song I remember best, the one that often pops into my mind unaccountably all these years later, is the wise man Balthazar's delighted uncovering of his never-empty magic box for young Amahl. "This is my box. This is my box," he whispers, his voice thrilling with secret delights, "I never travel without my box." It's a multi-drawered affair which contains everything a child could wish for, including "licorice, licorice, black sweet black sweet black sweet licorice." I can't remember exactly what I wanted in my own imagined magic box forty-two years ago. I always knew, of course, that I just couldn't count on any secret container to deliver all my heart's desires. But when I sit down at my desk these days, and see the three black and gold boxes of Maxell tapes that are tightly rubber-banded together in one corner, I recognize my own Balthazar's feast there — boxes containing my father's voice and the tales he told me, defining and refining the stories and memories of my own life, endlessly.

IX

SONS AND FATHERS, FATHERS AND SONS

Passing (It) On

My father approached his death, as he faced so much else in his life, with a strong sense of irony. Frustrated by the medicines he had to take every four hours for arthritis, for his heart, and to thin his blood, he'd announce: "I've got more pills in my drawer than a druggist." But he joked steadily, too, during our Sunday afternoon phone chats. While he let me know weekly that he was "still moving down the slippery slope of time," he'd talk mischievously about the joys of being buried in your car ("Man, that's living"), perhaps because he'd reached an age where giving up his driver's license after seventy years behind the wheel made sense to him. Or he'd share the pool-side black humor of a group that was shrinking every week. "Irwin told me a good one," he'd say, smiling over the phone lines. "It's about a guy who was visited by a dear, dead friend who announced the news from heaven: 'Herbie, Herbie, I've just been THERE,' the friend says, floating near the bedside. 'I've seen wondrous things — seen God and his angels, seen the gated city (it's not as secure as Leisure World, you better believe it), and I'm here to tell you that there's good news and bad news from up there. The good news — you're not gonna believe this — is that there's baseball in heaven. No, really! The bad news is that you're scheduled to be starting pitcher tomorrow.'"

I'd heard lots of this kind of talk when I visited Leisure World at Christmas. It was, I think, part of the bravado of diminished expectations among the octogenarian set. Death had become a steady fact of life for most of my parents' friends and acquaintances, and they faced it openly. Together with investment strategies, surgery procedures, and summaries of the lives of successful children, it was the most energetically pursued topic of conversation of those who sat in the overheated whirlpool baths.

My mother didn't participate much in the medical, financial, familial, or funereal exchanges, and my father kept to his laps in the pool. But I enjoyed the jet stream on my aching back, and enjoyed my realization that I was bathing outdoors while my friends back home were shoveling-out. My time in the whirlpool had been punctuated by my mother continually introducing me to the gang of seniors who'd sought solace in the steaming water. I explained again and again just where in upstate New York I lived, agreeing again and again that California was the place to be in winter and that Leisure World was the place to be in California. I confirmed that I had no stock market tips for myself or anyone, and I listened with muted concern to a litany of medical diagnoses. Once I even jumped out of the water to escort a skinny, addled man back to the locker room to reclaim the swim suit he didn't realize he'd forgotten to put on. But the memorable moment for me came when a bird-like, balding woman with a heavy Austrian accent looked up at me suddenly, and with surprise exclaimed that I was sitting exactly where Morris had landed in the whirlpool last week when he slipped out of his wheel chair and into the water, dead. It seems that one minute he had been in his usual spot parked above the water jets, looking on and smiling, when he'd gone limp and slowly slid feet first onto my very spot, as if inexorably drawn by the warmth and wet. They'd tried to revive him, but Morris was gone. She said it as if she could see him camped on my head and was a bit resentful at my having displaced him.

I was stuck for a proper response to this news. Though the woman was staggeringly matter-of-fact, and none of the others in the pool seemed concerned that I had replaced Morris, positionally, so to speak, this clearly had the potential to be felt as a senti-mental tragedy of near Dickensian proportions. As the conversation moved on, I could almost hear Dickens exclaim: "Dead! Right Reverends and Wrong Reverends of every order. Dead, men and women, born with Heavenly compassion in your hearts. And dying thus around us every day."

Dead, of course, but as Morris slid again and again from his chair into the bath, he was renewed and invigorated by memory and anecdote, and was prob-ably more alive in the week after his fatal stroke than he had been for months before. I developed an affection for the old man, whose presence reminded me that these days you don't "die," which is final, but "pass," which continues.

When I hear the word, I instantly see lines of ghostly students with their pencils sharpened for a big exam, or, even more absurdly, an assembly filled with celebrant corpses who have completed a course and are moving, with their white corsages, over to the next grade for further study. But mostly, since my father died on April Fool's day of last year, the absurd euphemism, persistently hissing in my mind at the oddest moments, has left me pondering my experience of having received a legacy of family memory, continuity, and connection together with a strongly felt sense of the responsibility to pass it on to my own sons. It came to me wrapped in feelings and actions which have become exemplary tales. What now, I wonder, has passed with my father's passing? What should I tell my sons? What do they want to hear?

The Bunk

"History is more or less the bunk," Henry Ford told his fellow Americans back in 1919. "It is tradition. We don't want tradition. We want to live in the present, and the only history that is worth a tinker's dam is the history we make today."

Like most young men, my sons used to say things

like that — even before they'd driven one of Henry's Fords. But lately they've both begun, quietly, to show an interest in the past as something of worth that you take with you rather than an annoyance to be sloughed off and left behind in pursuit of the present.

With my older son now working as an editor and journalist in Helsinki, and my younger busy with his life as a musician in Boston, we don't get much chance to sit down together for easy conversation. While we're in touch often, cyber-chatting with email, or building an eye-popping Sprint bill, our communication is usually focused on money matters, job complaints, commonplaces. But when my twenty-six-year-old comes home for a quick visit with his new wife, and his brother hops a bus up from Bean Town for the weekend, we find ourselves one evening roaming in the pastures of our intertwined histories and memories.

Worrying

Offering no casual chatter to ease me into the question, my younger son wants to know when his mother and I decided that we wanted to have children. He tells me that a friend of his has just had a baby, and that she's beautiful, but she's a hell of a big commitment. There are so many other things he wants to do. He wonders how anyone gets anything done. He says he can't imagine it for himself.

I guess my boys were just easy babies, I tell him, laughing. And parenting offered the reward of worry. How can you say no to that? But I find his question unsettling. I've always assumed, without thinking much about it, that my kids would want children. Wouldn't anyone raised in a nurturing environment? Having kids is what you do when you grow up; it's cultural, anthropological, mythic. I fret that his open declaration of not wanting them reflects somehow a kind of personal failure of my fathering. For more than a quarter of a century I've defined myself primarily as a parent, and the fact is I just don't know why I started down that path, or how I've negotiated the twists and turns. But I'm only partly kidding about the pleasures of worrying.

Trying to explain, I ask if he remembers a visit to his grandmother and granddad in Arizona when he was small. One afternoon we drove out to the Grand Canyon and walked along one of the rims. There were signs everywhere warning us to keep children back from the edge. But the boys were off like a shot. There was a fence part of the way along the walk, and maybe they knew enough to stop short of that anyway. But my wife and I took out after them, caught up in a few steps, and for the rest of the time wouldn't let go of their hands. We didn't see much of the Canyon, but the truth is it felt good to be hold-ing on.

There was pleasure in facing the fear that some-thing might go wrong, and beating it; in thinking about sore throats, ear infections, schoolwork, soccer goals, friendships, instead of grinding about committee meetings, administrative decisions, ugly politics in the workplace. It was a kind of productive worrying.

My older son was a feisty kid, always restless, even in his sleep. He slept face down, with his legs up under him and his arms pulled in, all bunched together like a spring ready to snap open. My younger was as loose as his brother was tight. He'd lie on his back with his head lolling to the side, just zonked and gone to the world. But they both managed to catch our attention whenever they wanted to, and sometimes when they definitely didn't. It seemed those first years that we'd wind up at least once a month pointing our car toward the Children's Hospital Emergency Room, hauling one or the other of them, or both, down for a stitch, or a shot, or at the very least a look-over. We collected antibiotics like gummy balls. Our medicine cabinet was filled with bottles of grape flavored cough syrup. My wife and I felt completely responsible, completely involved. Worrying became habitual, and helped us understand what mattered.

"You probably don't remember your first stitches," I say to my first born, "seeing as how your body has become a map of hockey and rugby scars." But those same scars that chart my son's life journey of forgetting, keep fresh my own memory of his first scars, his first childhood crisis. He was in the little bedroom off the attic, just waking up from a nap, entertaining his brother. I was working downstairs, and I could hear the little one laughing while his older brother made silly noises. Then there was total silence. It was so quiet after so much noise, that I came upstairs to see what was up. His grandmother used to say that the time to really worry was when kids were together and there wasn't a sound. There he was, covered in blood; his pillow was bloody, and his blanket. He'd been bouncing up and down in his crib, much to his brother's delight, and he'd hit his head coming down on the sharp edge of the bed frame. I'd never seen him so still. Maybe he was in shock. The blood was in his hair, his eyes; his pajamas were stained with it. I was yelling for his mother, grabbing him, trying to figure out where the wound was, and what had happened, holding a towel against his face to stop the bleeding. He only began to cry when he felt my own fear. Then he was quiet again.

A friend of ours came over to watch his little brother, while his mother and I bundled him into the car and took off for the hospital. He was totally silent for the whole drive, and completely still. His mother held him and talked softly in his ear, saying that we'd get him fixed up right away. Even when the doctor hustled him into surgery, and covered his head with a sheet that allowed him to isolate the cut, exposing it through a hole in the cloth, my son didn't move, didn't speak or cry. Not when the doctor gave him a shot for the pain. Not when he began to stitch the deep jagged tear along the top of his forehead, using a thick needle and thread, as if the boy was a deflated soccer ball being patched. After the doctor was done, though, my son chattered non-stop. On the drive home he looked out the window and offered running commentary on every store we passed, every person, every house, every green lawn, every car on the road. He asked us if he would always have the stitches in his head. He wondered what we were going to have for supper, and where his brother was. It was as if he had come back to the world after a long sleep. His mother and I felt, for the moment, like we had all been rescued, and that the world was a terrific place.

"Well, you'd expect him to get into trouble," my younger son laughs, "but not me, eh?"

I reassure him that he was more cautious, very careful, in fact, at least until he was about twelve and contrariness hit with a vengeance. While his older brother always seemed able to put us off by doing most of what was expected by authority figures, usually accompanying his actions with muttered sarcasms like "hey, whatever," he would have none of it. In fact, he was a real challenge to the concept of worthwhile worry.

A Little High Knee Action

Thinking that night about my younger son's occasionally bumpy growing up, I found myself remembering what my father used to say to me when things didn't seem to go right. "All you can do is give it your best," he'd exclaim, "and after that, whatever happens, happens." Sometimes when I was a kid, he'd follow it up with "the longest climb begins with a single step." Or he'd remind me to "put one foot in front of the other and provide a little high knee action." I suppose it was a nurturing mix of his protective parental concern and his pep talks as a high school track coach. We both knew it was Americana hokey, but I liked it, and took comfort in it while I worked things out with my tiny demons of achievement and ambition.

Like most of the kids I grew up with, I was goal oriented and fear driven. I suppose I knew I wouldn't fail too badly, that my "best" would be good enough to save my face with my other smart friends; but the thought that all I really had to do was fight the good fight helped. The line wasn't needed for my older son. He moved apparently without fear through the same sort of science heavy curriculum that had sent me into a post-sputnik funk in my student days; he played all sports with absurd abandon; and his favorite expression after a time became a flip, neutralizing, "as you say, master," whenever I planted a seed of what I saw as caution and reason, and which he dismissed as dangerous doubt. Nor did it seem likely to help my younger son, who, when it came to pushing on through to the end of a task deemed appropriate for a young lad with worlds to conquer — activities which all members of my family had performed, though perhaps without much relish — simply balked, and like Melville's Bartleby, "preferred not to" and would not be moved.

My wife and I had our first sharp reality check about him during the fall "Parent's Night" of his freshman year of high school. He had come back neo-punk restless from our family's six months of living in England. His theatrically black spiked hair, tame by Trafalgar Square standards, had been outrageous and shocking to most upstate sensibilities; and the habit that followed of wearing it full over his face seemed to irritate each and every adult whose path he crossed.

Trudging the halls of our city's one large public secondary school, my wife and I found ourselves entertained with the first choruses of what was to be the old sad song of our year. We weren't quite surprised, though not quite prepared, either. What those of his teachers who had registered my son's existence wanted to know was what was he hiding behind his hairy mask? Was he sleeping there? Plotting? Reveling in unspoken sinister sarcasm? Stoned or drunk? Did I know what it was like trying to follow monosyllabic grunts without making lip or eye contact? Did I know? What could I say? It made them uncomfortable. It made me uncomfortable. But it was a declaration of difference that would not be wished or willed away.

Like a child who'd been caught-out, I felt nervously apologetic for allowing my personal representative to the life of the mind to trouble these hard working educators — felt guilty, that is, until I realized that the bottom line for most of them was not to work it out, work with him, but simply to let me know that they weren't about to put up with his sullen and hostile presence. He'd either shape up or be gone. They didn't have time for this crap. What I wanted desperately to know was what would emerge from this cocoon, and when; if there was anything I could be doing to speed up the transformation process, and if my nerves could take the metamorphic wait.

What flashed before me that night, my middle-aging bulk squeezed into the unforgiving desks, were fragments of the ruins of my own early educating. At P.S. 94 I'd spent what seemed like whole uninterrupted years banished into the class clothing closet, pressed up against wet wool winter coats and rancid rubber boots; it was the reward for inattention. Being let out didn't improve things much. In gym class, when we weren't dribbling basketballs endlessly as we stood in place, our regular default activity was marching. While some orderly, well-coordinated good soldiers showed off their crisp rhythm, I didn't seem to be able to make much sense out of "to the rear march." Turning late, or early, or in the wrong direction, I was a stumbling embodiment of the domino effect we'd hear so much about years later. By the time I'd faced about, my part of the army of innocents was sure to be in disarray, a result which our General, Mrs. Cohen, seemed to take personally every time. Finally, when she couldn't stand it anymore, and her shouting passed to shrieking, she took out after me, blowing her whistle for me to stop while she waved her umbrella in threatening wide arcs above her head. I kept moving, of course — a good educational impulse, observing my father's "high knee action" advice as literally as I could. But all roads, it seemed, led back to the clothing closet, where I could only settle down once again in the mildewed damp, like a twice-caught POW, to wait out the learning wars.

Mrs. Hawker was a worse nightmare. Commonly known as "the Hawk" because of the way her sharp, predatory features and keen, killing eye fit the poetic possibilities of her name, she regularly teased and tortured the students who were her mouse-like prey. The Hawk's hard stare fixed on you was invariably followed by her claw-like hand pulled slowly from the pocket of her utilitarian gray cardigan sweater. Circling the air, signaling ruination for some targeted graceless, watery-eyed small beast, it would come to rest with a sharp jerk — pointing, demanding, accusing: "You!" To complicate matters, the threatening finger that emerged from the fist was forever bent into a right angle, probably twisted by arthritis or some more obscure disease of the spirit. Whether to observe the line at the first joint, then, or to follow around the bend and go with the final direction of the fingertip, determined just who was the targeted victim of the moment. Because of the ambiguity, everyone to the front and to the left of Mrs. Hawker's extended right hand was invariably swept up in the accusation. Whole rows of students were implicated in the attack; figuratively speaking they pissed their pants in fear, acknowledged guilt of unknown crimes against the system, awaited punishments which ranged from a clout upside the head and hands rapped with a metal ruler, to an extra two hours after school, time well spent reflecting on past sins both of commission and omission. It was nothing personal, of course. Mrs. Hawker was just fulfilling her part of the natural process, helping us all to survive what Charles Darwin once deemed the "Struggle for Life" leading to "Natural Selection, entailing Divergence of Character and the Extinction of less-improved forms." Drawing out our cunning in response to fear, our quiescence in response to intimidation, our capacity for disguise in the face of public exposure, the Hawk improved us.

Mrs. Sligo, the third of the weird sisters of my schooling, was, as they say, a horse of another color. Though she too had blue hair pulled into a don't-mess-with-me bun — the schoolmarm's badge — and she must have been as solidly built as the wrestler Andre the Giant, she seemed not to share her colleagues' impulse toward malevolence. She simply had the misfortune to teach the sewing shop class to a group of misplaced boys. We were part of a city school experiment that put boys in a seven week cooking class followed by the same again of sewing. I didn't mind; my efforts in the "manly" crafts had never gone well. The fishing tackle box I'd tried to bend and hammer into shape in a metal-working class had stimulated my teacher to observe that I worked like a fart in a gale; and though I thought I'd followed instructions perfectly, working from a book called *Electrical Things Boys Like to Make*, I found that I couldn't make the simplest project in the book, a telegraph that worked. My rocker arm rocked down but not up unless I flicked it free of the magnetic coil with my finger. I had made a machine that was capable of dashes but no dots, longs without shorts — not much use for encoded messages of distress. But cooking at least ended with tuna casserole; and sewing seemed like an appropriate dip into the family trade embodied by my grandfathers, the tailor and the cutter.

Lord knows my project seemed simple enough: a pink apron for my mother, with three large pockets for holding clothespins, so that when the spring and summer came back to the Bronx she could put the wash up to dry on the line that stretched across the roof of our apartment house. I was pleased that I might actually accomplish something I could recognize as useful. What happened was a disaster beyond anything I'd experienced or imagined.

The day I was finally ready to pull things together was the day things fully came apart. Each of us had a heavy iron Singer sewing machine, formidable things like battleships due for retirement, that had probably been used in garment district sweat shops for decades before being tossed out to the city school system. They were pedal driven, and while you sat and stitched it was possible to fantasize playing the Hammond organ with your favorite R&B band, or putting the pedal to the metal in a car; the act of basic sewing didn't seem to require too much concentration, and offered a fine chance to mind-wander. Which is probably how I got into trouble.

Classes usually began with a ritual five minutes of pin throwing, a boys-will-be-boys event that Mrs. Sligo generally managed to turn away from by burrowing into her closet for materials, looking around only when one of us dramatically yelped as a pin stuck in an arm or neck. But this was my day to hem and attach the large pink front of the apron to the thin cloth band, also pink, that would run across it and tie in the back. I could almost see the appreciation on my mother's face as she climbed up to the roof and dug into those large pink pockets that would hold dozens and dozens of useful clothespins. And I looked forward at last to finishing *something* made, more or less, with my own two hands. It was not as solid as a tackle box, but at least it wouldn't be used to carry weapons to kill fish; it was not as complex as a telegraph, but who used those anymore anyway? There would be no more gas in a gale, spit into the wind jokes — just the solid, satisfying, end of a project. Which is why I was engrossed immediately when the class began, skipping the delights of the aerial pin attacks; which is why Mrs. Sligo, turning outward from her supply closet, chose to notice me, and came over to check out my accomplishments. All would have been well had Mrs. Sligo not chosen this day to wear her baggy pink dress. And even so, I might have managed to get through the moment unscathed had I not mixed mind wandering with needle speed as I ripped the machine quickly through its joining task while imagining myself "Up On the Roof" with the Drifters, where, as the song goes, "it's peaceful and serene"; and with Marlon Brando, who as far as I know never wore an apron to feed his pigeons; and with my mom. I was simply not paying attention when Mrs. Sligo leaned over to inspect my work, suffocating me in the heavy smells of her mixed sweat and body talc, confusing me with her looming presence. Startled, suddenly self-conscious, I kept my head down and my Singer ratatating along, and found after a few minutes that my apron was "whole" at last, one lovely sewed together unit. I found too, to my surprise, that as Mrs. Sligo finally left to circulate among my less engaged friends, my apron was leaving with her. Of course, seeing my project slip down off my sewing table generated the only proper response: I slammed my hand down on the table to keep it in place. I grabbed the cloth and held it fast. How was I to know that in my absent-minded haste to finish the apron I had sewn Mrs. Sligo's pink dress to my mother's pink apron, and that in leaving she was dragging my project down with her? Or that holding tight to what was, after all, mine, I would tear Mrs. Sligo's dress broadly down the side and back? In retrospect, I was pleased to discover that my mother's apron emerged untorn, surely a sign of my having learned my lessons well.

I joined in the class laughter as a way of deflecting confusion and embarrassment. Mrs. Sligo was, as they say of Queen Victoria, not amused. My project grade was 45; my final grade was F-. But my mother wore that apron until well past my years in high school.

Of course I'd had good teachers too, outnumbered by the burnt-out or never-fired. But sitting in my son's parent-filled classrooms, listening against my will to the self-satisfied droning and buzzing coming from up-front, I recognized that the qualities which had brought me through the city school system relatively undamaged were a sense of the rules, a desire to please, patience and caution. I ached for my younger son lacking these, and my stomach knotted with my inability to know how to help a child who just would not play the game as the rules demanded.

Don't Try to Find Me

Inch by inch, all during the autumn and long winter, the lines between parent and child were drawn sharper, darker, deeper. My wife and I tossed our son some slack, then, uncomfortable with our abandonment of roles and responsibilities, pulled tighter. We squabbled about whether we'd all sit down cheerfully to family dinners, and about what time he'd come home. We went head to head about phone calls at late hours, about doing homework and household chores, about the herds of large young people flopped in what had been adult spaces, *our* spaces. Shrill fits and fierce silences chased each other through the house.

There was no lack of oral history in the family to turn to for wisdom — yarns about black sheep uncles, aunts, brothers, sisters, who'd settled down and made good. But the tale telling always seemed to focus less on the triumphant return of the prodigal, than on juicier woeful stories of lost relatives who disappeared or went crazy, rode the rails into oblivion, slid onto skid row, turned up in lower east side flop houses. Not much for edification there.

My parents and in-laws assured us that all this was normal, to be expected, not to be much fussed about. And when I asked my father how he'd handled *his* kids in their difficult time, he breezed by it with "What difficult time? There was nothing to handle." Perhaps he'd never really noticed; perhaps he had selective memory; perhaps we were, in his eyes, "good." But though comforting, his easy-going grandparental attitude was not what we needed.

Moving beyond a search for family lore, my wife and I, modern parents, sought answers and solace in our HMO's parent rap group. We learned that the battle lines were drawn all over town, and that others had it worse. We learned also that the answers in the dynamic parenting book we'd bought ahead of the class were about as valuable as Bill Cosby reruns. Cute cartoons told us how to be sympathetic and productive listeners. On the loose-leafed large format pages, frowny faces gave way to smiley faces, as moms and dads in sporty leisure wear and kids in funky T-shirts wrestled out heady issues like what to do when the borrowed family car is dented, or when you find your daughter's cigarettes, your son's beer. Warm exclamations of parental empathy, it seemed, were to precede declarations of how it was, and how it was to be — a sucker punch followed by a knockout punch. They called it productive listening: "I know you must be upset... I can see that we all need time to think it over." But that didn't help the couple sitting across from us in the small tight circle, whose adopted son was unhappy with his parents, and was fast becoming a school and family drop out; it didn't help the stepmother who, while her second husband was off drinking in the evening, was left to deal with his huge and surly sons. And it didn't help us.

"I'm OK, but I'm not coming home tonight. Don't try to find me." Slam. That's how the night of the runaway began. Oh, hell, "I know you must be upset..." We were left to talk into the dead receiver, one of the drawbacks of "productive listening." We knew that he really was OK — no deprivation, no physical danger, probably hanging out at his friend Jack's, skate boarding on the quiet dark streets, talking serious talk and feeling sorry for himself and self-righteous. But we weren't confident enough about what might be next, and we couldn't let it be. We felt stuck in a comic strip, with clear vision but no way out as we hit the street to search for him.

My mother tells me that I almost ran away once, miffed by some slight at the age of seven. She helped me get my red wool coat out, my fuzzy earflap hat, my thick blue knit scarf, a bag crammed with essential toys. And having let me dress up to go out, she hit me with the stopper. Maybe I'd like to run away after supper, after macaroni and a chance to listen to the latest Sky King on the radio. I wouldn't want to miss the secret message from Sky, would I? That's what my decoder ring was for, after all. Better to run on a full stomach, she said, and I said OK. On a full stomach, of course, you don't run, you barely walk. And so I sounded my litany as my wife and I headed out into the dark all those years later: linguini, macaroni — eat a little, kid, then take it on the road — we'll both feel better, eh?

But my son was not seven, bundled like Charlie Brown against the cold, and easily bought off or backed off. If truth be told, it was a rotten night, the kind that sticks in memory, and it was unpunctuated by any pasta relief. Still, we got home together after a while and began to find our ways.

Standing in the kitchen at midnight, squeezing a can shaped lump of orange juice concentrate into a white stoneware pitcher that was almost heavy enough to require a two hand lift, I argued stupidly with my son about proper behavior. Now, I'm not much given to epiphanic moments — even a predictable classroom discussion of a Joycean epiphany has always struck me as a survey of self-willed make believe; but that night I was graced with a surprising, loud, wet, "Aha! phenomenon." Thinking about how jerked around I felt as I stirred the OJ, I surprised myself by slamming the pitcher down onto the table like an exclamation point to mark with emphasis and passion some obvious complaint. The grand wave of orange juice that washed over us both, and the shards of broken pottery lying on the floor in a sticky mess, shocked us into speechlessness, then laughter, and finally renewed calm from which ego seemed for a moment to have broken away. In the late night silence, punctuated only by the slap and squeak of sticky sneakers as we went about our clean up, we found that we could fill the air with talk.

Onward and Upward

With the tight fist of the season and our mood unclenching, my son and I began to spend days on the road, driving down into the valleys of the rich to spend time at places that neither of us had the slightest notion of: boarding schools, where we hoped he could find some pleasure in learning before he was lost to education forever. I thought vaguely of born teachers and small classes gathering on grassy hillsides for intense, intimate discussions about art and history. I thought, too, of horses and hounds, Tom Brown's school days, E.M. Forster's white-jacketed languorous young men. I should have been thinking Calvin Klein, J.Crew. My childhood had come trailing some very un-Wordsworthian clouds of union rhetoric, tracings from my grandfathers' Garment Workers Union slogans and their contempt for the monsters who hovered dangerously near the ordinary guy, ready to destroy us all: the bosses. And here I was driving right through the gates of privilege where bosses were groomed. I could almost feel my grandfathers' bones grinding as I stood in front of bulletin boards, reading about the doings of name-recognition grads who dwelt in castles in compounds near water, ruled companies, flew the Concorde across the pond for recreational leisure.

What you see is what you get. Solid American wisdom. Together we saw one place that would do. There was privilege alright, but it didn't reek of it. It reeked, in fact, of cow manure, and all students were expected to shovel shit at early a.m. barn duty, working an active farm as they worked their minds. They were scholar-farmers — Crevecoeur would have been proud. For three years my son chopped and planted, shoveled and raked, hammered and painted, while memorizing, arguing, writing, performing. I think my grandfathers would have approved — the making not of bosses, but the unbossed.

Years later, working as a waiter, a musician, and a returning college student near the end of schooling at last, and getting ready to write his final papers, our not-so-young son sent us a joking and plaintive email. Trying to lift the considerable weight of his readings in "Victorian Fiction," "Ethics," "Great Books," "Cultural Anthropology," and "Classical Philosophy" he wrote, simply, "Help. I need a rub." Parental back rubs had solved a lot over the years, from the earliest days when, as a toddler, he'd climb up on our laps for a quick nuzzle and squeeze, to later when he'd suddenly present himself — six foot three, not counting the extra lift from his Doc Martens — push aside the book I was reading, park himself on the couch next to me and say, "how about some help with tension release. I *really* could use a back rub, dad." It was a ritual of connection I loved and I was glad to oblige, but there was no way I could massage him from England where my wife and I were living for awhile. Still, sitting down at my Zenith lap top, I tapped out my message of coherence, continuity, remembrance, offering a figurative rub for the spirit from father to son and father to son again: "Dear T, remember what Grandpa used to say, all you need to do — all you *can* do — is put one foot in front of the other and provide a little high knee action. Look for a rub when we get home at Christmas; I'll start with the knees, I promise."

Photos

As I reach for the box of family photos that I've gotten down from a high closet shelf sometime during
the evening of talk and thought, I tell my sons that
from year one they put their mother and me in
touch with memories of our own pasts, and, like
never before, brought us close to their grandparents
who'd been through it all and could always let us
know that we would come to the delight at the end
of every dark tunnel of worry.

"Someday you'll have children of your own," my
mother used to say to me when I was particularly
ill mannered or disobedient, as if that would be just
punishment enough and she could hardly wait. But
I think she knew that when I did, I would not only
remember her admonitions, but that in the process
I'd rediscover myself as part of the family's continuity in a way that I couldn't even imagine in those
long lost days before I had children.

"Look at us," I say, hauling out the old photographs
so that we can tour the family generations together.
We observe my bantam-weight grandfather dressed
in a dark suit on the beach at Rockaway, stiff and
indifferent to the swimmers and volleyball players
who find some fun at the water's edge around him;
and my sad grandmother sitting on her bench in
Van Cortlandt Park, squinting into the camera —
once a formidable presence, but now fading into the
white of the bleached snapshot. My worried-looking

step-grandmother and my dapper, sweet-smiling step-grandfather stand beside each other in front of their Bronx apartment, not touching. My young father comes into focus, bare-chested and muscled, playing tennis, and then my worn out father, sixty years later, his eyes still lively with affection, but thin-faced and tired in a blue golf hat that appears to be sizes too large for him. My mother, hating to be photographed, stands with him, energetic and nautical in her blue sailor's blouse and sporty white pleated skirt. My wife, black hair sharply contrasting her white dress, and I with my hair cut so short that my ears stick out like coat hooks, look dazedly into the distance on our wedding day. Then there they are, tiny versions of their grown selves, but completely recognizable, my older son with his arm around my younger. They stand at the back door peering into the dark of the house, quizzical but impatient to be on their way.

Throughout the rest of the night, we each in turn, when we can, add voice to the still lives, asking questions, supplying anecdotes and family narratives. While we shuffle our deck of photo cards, and talk with pleasure about what has passed and what remains, it's clear that for each of us, what is *now* is indelibly marked by what, having been, will always, to some extent, *be*.

Keeper

When my father mailed me his three large reel-to-reel tapes of conversations with my grandfather nearly thirty years ago, I reacted like a book collector. Thrilled to have them, I quickly wrapped them in plastic for posterity and put them on an attic bookshelf where they'd be safe. I had asked for them, of course, and I treasured my grandfather's words, hoarded them. But the tapes discomforted me. I knew that I was the keeper of a sort of family treasure, and had a responsibility to protect it. Years later, I recognized that perhaps I wasn't protecting my grandfather's story, so much as protecting myself from the distraction of looking back through family history.

Some twenty-five years later when I put my own taped conversations with my father beside my grandfather's in the attic, I found myself thinking with confusion and distress that to play them would somehow be to signal my father's death, substituting his fixed, captured voice for his living voice. I feared too, though, that by letting the tapes gather dust I was simply on my way to becoming a keeper of the family crypt. When at last I pulled the conversations and stories out to play them, heard the voices pronouncing my grandfather's aggressive declaration of self, his insistent "I am," and my father's sweetness and patient humor — when I began to mix them with the cacophony of my grandmothers' lamentations and regrets, and my own

memories and imaginings — I found at last the res-
onances of my own voice, distinct but never solitary.
It marks me an inheritor and progenitor as clearly
as any gallery of photographs displaying my grandfather's small chin, my father's vanishing hairline,
my grandmother's troubled, sad smile, my older
son's confident stare, or my younger's easy grin.

My grandfather, who had every one of his teeth
firmly in his head when he died, used to say "you
can't chew with someone else's teeth," which I took
to mean be yourself, do it yourself, do it your way.
But he also would regularly offer for wisdom, "one
link snaps and the whole chain falls apart." These
always struck me as odd together, but hearing his
voice again and again, declaring the substance of his
hard life well-lived, I've come to find the combina-
tion logical and salutary. Listen, he seems to say, listen to the voices of your life — to what they say and
how they say it, and you will be able to bite down
hard without snapping through the chain of experience, of stories, of actions, of memories, that are the
links of our individual lives.

About the Author

Photo by Anastasia Pease

Harry Marten was born in New York City, raised in the Bronx, educated at Harpur College and the University of California at Santa Barbara. He teaches modern and contemporary literature at Union College in Schenectady, New York, where he is the Edward E. Hale, Jr., Professor of English and Chair of the English department. He has published in *The New York Times Book Review*, *The Washington Post Book World*, *The Gettysburg Review*, *The Ohio Review*, *New England Review*, *The Cortland Review*, and others; and he has written books on Conrad Aiken and Denise Levertov. Married, with two grown sons, he lives in Niskayuna, New York, with his wife, Ginit.